Happy Bir
Much Lov
Steven & Jo

1991

G000089300

# Historic WIGAN

*Two thousand years of history, by John Hannavy*

**Cover illustration** — *The Dinner Hour, Wigan, by Eyre Crowe. Reproduced by kind permission of Manchester City Art Galleries.*

*Carnegie Publishing,*
1 9 9 0

*For Eileen,*

*who encouraged me for twenty years*

*Historic Wigan*
by John Hannavy

First edition, November 1990
Published by Carnegie Publishing Ltd., 18 Maynard Street, Preston PR2 2AL
Designed and typeset in Caslon Antique and Times Medium by Carnegie Publishing Ltd.
Printed and bound in the UK by Leyland Printing Co. Ltd., Leyland Lane, Leyland, Lancashire

**ISBN 0 948789 58 1**

# Contents

## About the author

JOHN Hannavy is a well-known writer and broadcaster, and the author or co-author of several other books about Wigan – dealing mainly with the photography of Wigan over the last 150 years. Dr Hannavy studied photographic technology in Manchester in the 1960s and since then has worked in Manchester, Wigan and Bolton. He has researched and organised major exhibitions on photographic history and written extensively on the subject.

He has lived in Wigan for the last twenty years and works in Bolton where he is Head of Art & Design and Bolton Institute of Higher Education.

# Acknowledgements

THIS book could not have been completed without the help of a great many people over the years, all of whom have brought illustrations to my attention, allowed me to copy material from their collections, or extended my knowledge of the history of Wigan. To them all, my thanks are due.

Many of the pictures come from my own collection built up over the years, and over the production of five earlier books about Wigan. Many others have been supplied by Wigan Heritage Service from their collections. To these I have added my own modern photographs to illustrate aspects of the town's past, present and future.

To my co-authors on some of those earlier projects, Roy Lewis, Jack Winstanley and Chris Ryan, I owe my thanks for their expertise and collaboration, and an acknowledgement that at least some of the historical information contained in this work was researched jointly. The Library & Learning Resources Department at Bolton Institute, and Wigan Reference Library have also helped by getting hold of material for me.

Thanks also go to Mrs Helen Aldred, Beryl Moss, William Millard, the Reverend Malcolm Forrest and his team of helpers at Wigan Parish Church, the Station Supervisors and staff at British Rail Wigan North Western, British Coal and the staff of Raymin (Northern) Ltd. at the Alexandra Open Cast site, Geoffrey Shryhane and Alan Rimmer at the *Wigan Observer*, Nick Webb, Len Hudson and Sally Coleman of Wigan Heritage Service, and to Alastair Gillies for his continued help and support for any project which brings Wigan's past to the notice of today's readers.

Last, but by no means least, thanks to Alistair Hodge at Carnegie Publishing for giving me the excuse to do some of the most fascinating research I have done for some time!

*John Hannavy*
Wigan, October 1989

# Introduction

TANDING at the top of Standishgate, near Mabs Cross, and looking back down towards the town centre, it is hard to imagine two thousand and more years of history having been played out within the area visible before you. For, so extensive was the redevelopment of the town in the nineteenth and twentieth centuries that very little evidence remains to suggest a long and glorious past.

And yet, within the few square miles which made up the old County Borough of Wigan before local government reorganisation fifteen years ago, a sequence of events which coloured and influenced the history of England itself was played out over the preceding twenty centuries. They may not have been the major events in most instances, but they were nonetheless, in their way, influential in the development of a nation.

Like so many other towns of similar size and importance, the early history of Wigan was much more visible a century and a half ago than it is today. The development of heavy industry, of factories, railways and the infrastructure of a booming nineteenth-century town swept much away in the nineteenth century.

The development of Wigan's railway stations, the gasworks and the canal cut through much of the wealth of early historical remains, losing it forever. In the early to mid-nineteenth century, enthusiasm for carefully recording sites before they were developed was still a long way in the future. Thus, while Roman coins, early pottery and other artefacts of earlier civilisations were found and noted, little serious attempt was made to record them, their locations and their circumstances.

Much of the town's early history, therefore, has been the subject of repeated conjecture by historians over the past hundred and fifty years, with facts, opinions and educated guesses in some cases being repeated from one writer to another to such a degree that a suggestion by one writer becomes a fact to the next and so on.

Serious research into some of the statements made in the earlier histories of the town show them to be little more than (sometimes) inspired guesses by writers based on incomplete data. So obscure are some of the periods of Wigan's past that the true picture may never become clear. All or most of the potential sources of information have been lost.

While the later history of Wigan is well documented – and by 'later' read the second millennium – the first thousand years is not. The period of pre-Roman, Roman, early British, Saxon and early Christian development is sketchy to say the least. From the time of the establishment of the parish church, and the beginnings of accurate records, the picture is very different.

Thus any attempt to establish a history for the first ten centuries is based on fragmentary evidence and a lot of conjecture – the pieces of the jigsaw are few and seldom fit together.

This book does not set out to be a definitive history of the town – to do so would require much more space than is at the disposal of this writer. What it does set out to create, however, is a broad-brush picture of how Wigan developed into the town it is today, and to do so in a light and lively manner. History is worthless if it is uninteresting!

For a writer more used to the development of history through visual material, this book represents a departure of considerable proportions. The previous five books on Wigan's history in the nineteenth and twentieth centuries have had a wealth of photographic evidence upon which to draw. For the eighteen earlier centuries, B.P. – before photography – visual evidence is much less easy to get hold of. Much of the story must therefore be described rather than illustrated.

Today, Wigan stands in a pivotal position at the crossing of the north-south and east-west railways, in a triangle bounded by the main arterial motorways, and within easy striking distance of most parts of the country. Modern communications networks make its central location one of its key industrial attributes.

In the last century when travel, transport and communication were less easy and much less rapid, Wigan was a key location on the canal network. Thus industrial Wigan has always depended on its relationship with the transport infrastructure of the country for its commercial success.

In the earliest days of the town's existence, it was the same story. Indeed, Wigan probably developed from a green-field site because of the need for a town, commercial centre or garrison at a key point on a main north-south road.

It is the story of the development of that green-field site into today's large town that this book celebrates.

Chapter One

# Roman Wigan and beyond

**The only accession which the Roman Empire received during the first century of the Christian era was the province of Britain. In this single instance the successors of Caesar and Augustus were persuaded to follow the example of the former, rather than the precept of the latter . . . After a war of about forty years . . . the greater part of the island submitted to the Roman yolk. The various tribes of Britons possessed valour without conduct, and the love of freedom without the spirit of union. They took up arms with savage fierceness; they laid them down, or turned them against each other, with wild inconsistency; and while they fought singly, they were successively subdued.**

Edward Gibbon
Introduction to *The Decline and Fall of the Roman Empire* (1776)

HE first of many areas of uncertainty and controversy in the history of Wigan revolves around the size, purpose and importance of the town as a Roman settlement. Not only are we unsure about the exact role of the Roman settlement, but evidence is also distinctly lacking about the nature of the site itself when it was first occupied.

Did Wigan begin with the Romans? Whilst many sources seem to point towards the establishment of the Roman settlement as being the origin of today's large town, others clearly suggest that they merely occupied a site which was already well established as a civil settlement by the time they arrived. Indeed, so uncertain is the nature of the Roman settlement that for many years there was even a dispute over whether there ever was one here at all. The Roman settlement of *Coccium* has variously been assumed to have been at Wigan, Standish, Blackrod and, indeed, several other local locations.

While it is now well established and accepted that Wigan was indeed the Roman *Coccium,* the exact area covered by the settlement has never been accurately defined. In the early-nineteenth century, while construction work on the gas works, and later on the stations, was underway, pottery and Roman coinage were discovered, suggesting a possible site in the Wallgate, King Street and Darlington Street area, but insufficient information exists to determine any boundaries for that site.

Even the name *Coccium* presents problems. While the Roman *Coccium* certainly did exist, and now seems certain to have been Wigan, the name is not essentially a Roman one. The Celtic word 'cochion' or 'coccion' – believed to have meant 'red' – is insufficiently far removed from *Coccium* to be discounted as a root for the settlement's name. Given the predominance of red sand in much of the Wigan area, the name may well have a Celtic root suggesting 'red hill' or something similar, implying perhaps that a Brigantian settlement predated the Roman arrival, and that 'Coccium' is a Latinisation of the existing name for the settlement. The hill site surrounding the present-day parish church would certainly have been a ideal location for an early British settlement – easy to defend on all sides and with a ready supply of fresh water from the River Douglas. Sadly the same cannot be said of the river today!

If we therefore assume that the Romans occupied an existing settlement, we are then left with the problem of defining and describing the nature of that Roman site. It is variously described in encyclopaedias and histories as a fort, a post, a town or a settlement. Its perceived importance varies considerably depending upon which of those definitions is accepted. In truth, the role of *Coccium* in the Roman plan of things is so obscure that it may never be fully understood.

*The early history of the town can only be guessed at – but evidence of earlier civilisations has been found at various times, including many axe heads, arrow heads and other relics. This axe head is from the Neolithic period.*

While it is now clearly beyond dispute that there was a Roman presence, best guesses of what that presence was must fall far short of it being a Roman town. A military station of some importance – at least towards the end of the Roman period – is perhaps the most likely theory, with a civilian presence alongside it, but not necessarily Roman. If there was a pre-Roman settlement, the Roman garrison may have been developed in place of or alongside it.

The north of England was unknown territory to the Romans as late as half way through the first century AD. The great cities of *Deva* (Chester) and *Eboracum* (York) were developed well after the first thrust northwards. From about 50 AD to 80 AD, the Roman movement northwards was achieved only as a result of almost perpetual fighting. Such Roman settlements as were established in the North West were military in purpose, and few if any civilian settlements were established. After 80 AD, when Julius Agricola was in command, the military machine moved further north and then, and only then, was there a period of relative quiet behind the lines. By 100 AD the pattern of military and indeed civilian occupation of the area covered by present-day Lancashire and Cheshire was relatively well established, and a consolidation of the infrastructure – roads, towns, military and civilian settlements – in support of the forward troops, had been established.

Roman military history then entered a period when the Romans were coming under attack from several quarters at once. It is clear from recent archaeological excavations throughout the north of England that there was a reduction in the size of the forts. This period culminated in the great Hadrian's Wall, defining rather more clearly than ever before the limits of the lands in which the Romans felt civilisation prevailed.

*Coccium* was clearly a late Roman development. In the first century AD, Roman roads ran from *Deva* (Chester) to *Mamucium* (Manchester) and from *Mamucium* to *Bremetennacum* (Ribchester), coming nowhere near present-day Wigan.

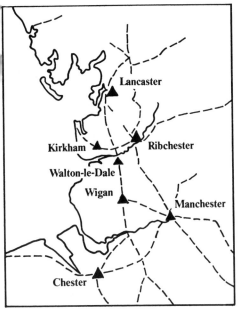

*The Roman roads of North West England.*

By around 100 AD, a new road had been driven through the Lancashire and Cheshire plains from a point just east of present-day Northwich, up through Wilderspool and Walton-le-Dale to Lancaster. It was that road which placed *Coccium* on the Roman map, but while Wilderspool and Walton-le-Dale are both known to have been civilian settlements with Roman garrisons, *Coccium's* role has never been as clearly defined. At this point in the development of the Roman transport infrastructure, it may well have been a Romanised civilian settlement guarding and protecting a key portion of the new north-south route.

Indeed, given the importance of Brigantian settlements such as Winwick in pre-Roman Britain, there is a very strong case for accepting the idea that the Romans adopted an earlier track or road and relaid it to their own standards. Additionally this would account for the meandering nature of the road, following the contours of the land rather than the Roman practice of driving a relatively straight line road from A to B.

*Coccium's* role, however, increased in importance considerably with the development of a much easier route north in the early part of the second century AD. The road north from *Mamucium* via the Ribble crossing at *Bremetennacum* can never have been easy for foot soldiers or for the heavy transports which kept the northern armies fed and clothed. The dating of that new road development is believed to have been approximately contemporary with the construction of the Roman wall. The easier route required the development of twenty miles of new road from *Mamucium* to *Coccium* to join up with the existing route north, and that placed *Coccium* in a much more important position within the road network. It now sat at a major junction, and it can be realistically assumed that from that moment onwards the Roman presence increased both in number and in strategic importance. The straight line of the new road additionally suggests that this was an entirely Roman route, not necessarily following an earlier track.

In establishing the routes of these two important roads, the best conjecture comes from nineteenth-century historians, whose researches were less hindered by two centuries of industrial development.

The main north-south road can be assumed to have followed approximately the route of the present A49 into the town – arriving at Wallgate and Market Place, perhaps with the civilian settlement to the north west and the Roman garrison to the south east, the latter occupying a site somewhere around that now occupied by North Western Station, and that previously occupied by the gas works.

While the road may have meandered through the countryside, the Romans would not normally have tolerated such a route near a garrison, town or settlement. Therefore, the present twists and turns of the A49 as it enters the town are almost certainly later deviations from the line of the Roman road. Straight lines were easier to defend, if not always as easy to construct. Whatever else the Romans did, their roads invariably approached their forts and garrisons directly.

Nineteenth-century historians traced the line of the east-west road through Hindley to a ford over the original line of the River Douglas somewhere about the bottom of Millgate. The junction of the two roads would, if that conjecture was accepted, be somewhere about the site of today's Market Place, and that might well, therefore, define the north-eastern limit of the Roman site.

These would have been paved roads – some ten metres wide with an area of cleared land to either side and, where necessary, defensive ditches some distance to either side of the paved way. The discovery of traces of this paving – alas now long lost – was recorded in the early years of the last century during the building of the main north-south railway line.

*In the eighteenth-century ceiling of the drawing room at Standish Hall, now demolished, Wigan's Roman past was remembered. A Roman soldier looked down from one of the panels, while his Emperor looked down from another panel in the same ceiling.*

By 142 AD, the Roman front line had been extended northwards to a line between the Rivers Forth and Clyde in Scotland, and *Coccium* was, therefore, that much further removed from the military frontier. For a considerable period of time, the lines held firm, and Roman Britain enjoyed a period of relative peace and stability.

The defeat of the native population of Brigantia by the Roman army was very effective and there was bitter revolt against the authority of Rome. At first Brigantia was a 'client kingdom' of Rome, a sort of very unequal partner, but once the area had been annexed by the Roman army, the effective military control of the area ensured considerable changes for the native British. Trade and inter-marriage led to the use of Latin whilst the tribal elite gradually became a 'romanised' hierarchy who undertook the main aspects of civilian administration.

Roman influence, in terms of civilisation, architecture, agriculture and general lifestyle, was felt far less heavily outside the central and south-eastern regions of England. Roman presence as far north as *Coccium* was predominantly military, with only whatever civilian support as was necessary for the service and support of the military garrison being tolerated. The absence of any evidence for notable civilian residences – towns or villas – north of Chester on the western side of the Pennines and York on the east, testifies to the essentially military nature of the Roman presence.

The townships which grew up at *Luguvallum* and *Corstopitum* on the Wall existed to support the garrisons, and can therefore not be classed as civilian settlements in the true sense. Recent excavations at Carlisle, however, have clearly demonstrated that this town was an important centre with a classical temple, a *mansio* (a sort of Roman hotel), a large centrally heated house as well as the strong possibility that the town had a *praetorium* building. Carlisle acted as a *civitas*, a native administrative and political centre, and amply demonstrates that even in the often hostile region of the north there was a degree of romanisation amongst the native British by the second century AD.

As far as Lancashire was concerned, the sixth legion, based at *Deva*, was perhaps the only major Roman presence between Chester and

*A Roman altar was unearthed during an eighteenth-century restoration of the parish church. At first it was built into the outside of the tower but in the nineteenth-century rebuilding of the church it was moved and set into a window recess inside the tower.*

Hadrian's Wall. However, there were significant units of the Roman army spread thinly across the north-west of England, especially at Ribchester and Lancaster which were both very important cavalry bases. Not for the northern peoples was there a sudden dawning of Roman civilisation, education, art and sophistication. That was reserved for the new breed of Romano-British in the Midlands, South and South East. The great buildings, bath-houses, mosaics and sculptures were as alien to the north west of England as they had ever been. No great Roman leaders ever ventured this far north, let alone lived here.

Equally, there is a complete absence of evidence to suggest that the Romans farmed the lands between *Coccium* and the sea. Had agricultural development on any scale taken place, the civil and administrative personnel drafted north in support of such activities would have left their marks by way of buildings, distribution centres and so on. What is much more likely is that their provisions were grown further south and hauled north across the network of roads. There was, however, a considerable increase in the level of industrial activity in the north as a response to the needs of the Roman army. Archaeological sites such as Wilderspool and Stockton Heath have produced evidence of considerable metal-working, pot and tile production and even glass making.

When the Romans eventually withdrew progressively further south, first the walls, and then the forts and military settlements which had supported them were abandoned. *Coccium* was no exception. It is possible that as with some of the old Roman forts and towns in the north and in the west that *Coccium* continued to be inhabited, and

*The so-called 'Boers Head Collection' of coins was discovered in the 1920s – a considerable collection of Roman coins covering the entire span of the Roman presence in the town. Their location at Boers Head might suggest that a signal station or mile station on the main north road was sited there. The coins are in very fine condition.*

certainly the decline in the settlement would have been gradual. Just what they left in terms of evidence of their presence will never be known. The passage of time has obliterated all of it long since. Indeed, as an essentially military settlement there may have been little of a substantial and permanent nature to leave, save for stone foundations upon which wooden buildings might have been constructed. Certainly the nineteenth-century romantic accounts of a derelict Roman town of *Coccium* being taken over by the first Saxons do not seem to have any basis in fact whatsoever.

The Romans withdrew from Britain in the first quarter of the fifth century – at first just transferring a legion or two to more troubled parts of the Empire and then, with too few troops to protect their strongholds in mainland Europe, they withdrew from Britain completely by about 430 AD. A combination of circumstances brought about the end of Roman Britain – circumstances which were more to do with the villa civilisation of the south than the military occupation of the north.

Whatever plans the Romans may have had for northern Britain – above a line from Chester to the Wash – were clearly never completed. While the natives were rendered relatively neutral in military terms, there was as we have seen little or no attempt to civilise them in true Roman terms. The northern provinces or cantons of Roman Britain may be seen in some ways as a buffer zone between the unruly Picts and Scots to the north and west, and the civilised Romans and

Romano-British in the south and east of the country.

By the end of the third century there was clearly the potential for trouble from the Scots. The Antonine Wall had first been abandoned before the end of the second century and rebuilt several times; Hadrian's Wall was the recognised northern frontier of Roman Britain.

If the Picts and Scots had ever acted as one, the Roman military command recognised that serious problems might ensue. That problem became a reality about 367 AD when the Picts from the North, the Scots from Ireland and the Saxons from northern mainland Europe, apparently working in concert, all descended upon Roman Britain at around the same time. The devastation they wrought was considerable and, although they were driven back beyond the frontiers of Roman Britannia, the beginning of the end had been signalled.

The Roman towns in the South had been badly damaged and when rebuilt were much more heavily fortified. A siege mentality quickly established itself and the once open and free lifestyle of the Romans and Romano-British became much more defensive in outlook. By the beginning of the fifth century, all Roman troops had been withdrawn and the Romano-British had been told to take steps to defend themselves without the protective umbrella of the Roman military machine. The Roman era had ended and for a time at least the tribal British of the Lancashire plain had the place to themselves again. The traditional image of a neat chronological sequence with the Romans leaving and the Anglo-Saxons arriving does not stand up to close scrutiny. While the Romans may have been influenced to leave by the Saxons, the Scots and the Picts, they were not immediately followed by them. It was the threat to civilised Britain further south which influenced the collapse of Roman Britain, and that happened a long time before the Saxons were in a position to settle in the south, and the Angles in the less hospitable areas of northern England.

The first Angles to cross the Pennines did so further north than Wigan, arriving some time in the sixth or early-seventh century. In that interim period, the British name of Wigan or some variation of that spelling probably returned to use, having been suppressed during three or four centuries of Roman control.

While the Anglii and the Saxons came from quite different parts of Europe, and settled in different parts of Britain, the period of their dominance of life and culture in Britain is generally given the collective title of Anglo-Saxon. With the Saxons initially in control in the south, and the Angles in control in the north, Britain entered a period of agricultural and village development on a much broader scale than had ever been countenanced by the Romans.

The Anglo-Saxons were valley-dwellers and farming property owners. It is therefore highly likely that the Anglian influence on the Wigan area was much greater in terms of the local economy than the Roman one had been. An Anglian – and later Anglo-Saxon – presence on the hills we now call Wigan would have been vastly different from the Roman one in many ways but not in others. Further south, the early years of this period have been identified with a loss of many of the civilising influences of Rome – a movement away from a written law, from order and from Christianity. Thus, the label of the 'Dark Ages' has a significance. Further north, there was little Roman light to be extinguished. There was no civilised infrastructure, only a military one. There had been little real romanisation of the ordinary native population, only control by the Roman army and a small romanised native elite.

In that respect, the advantages of Anglian rather than Roman control may well have outweighed the disadvantages. Despite their warrior zeal – a zeal which facilitated their widespread conquests – the newcomers were farmers and fishermen, and their agricultural development of the lands around Wigan, and between Wigan and the Mersey estuary, may well have brought the first instances of order to the area.

Hints as to where the first Anglian settlements were sited around Wigan might be gleaned from place names. Thus Billinge has a strong Anglian root – the 'inge' suffix on the name is derived from the Anglian 'inga', and Billinge is usually accepted as meaning something like the 'home of the hill people'. It could be argued, however, that Billinge was not an Anglo-Saxon settlement at all, but a settlement of the tribal British, identified as 'hill people' in the Anglian name. Confusions and varieties of interpretation abound, and will continue to do so, in the absence of any contemporary records.

However scarce relics of the Roman period might be, evidence of the Anglo-Saxon period is even scarcer. Their influence survives really only in place names, with little other tangible proof of their presence. In addition to Billinge, Worthington, Adlington and Pennington all show Anglian rather than native British influences in their names.

Wigan, on the other hand, does not, but that in no way serves to dismiss its importance in post-Roman England. It is, indeed, highly likely that the invaders took over the British settlement or town we now know as Wigan. It is equally likely that, with a return to Christianity in the seventh and eighth centuries, a church was built in Wigan. But centuries elapsed between the departure of the Romans and the erection of that first church. The Roman temple seems to have been somewhere near the site of the present parish church, because part of a Roman altar was discovered there in the eighteenth century and was incorporated into the tower during one of a sequence of restorations. Between the abandonment of the Roman fort and the erection of the first Christian church, however, several Anglian temples or places of worship may well have occupied the same site!

The scarcity of Anglo-Saxon relics in Lancashire in general is hardly surprising. The Anglians built of wood and wattle rather than stone, with straw-thatched roofs. Thus the buildings themselves were short-lived, and usually the only tangible proof of Anglian settlements is in their 'middens' or rubbish heaps, when archaeologists are lucky enough to discover them. It was not until the seventh century that building in stone became at all common, and even then, with the reappearance of a more formal Christianity, only for churches.

Chapter Two

# Into the light

After this had the King a large meeting and very deep consultation
with his council, about this land; how it was occupied and by what sort
of men. Then he sent his men all over England into each shire;
commissioning them to find out how many hundred of hides were in
the shire, what land the King himself had, and what stock was upon
the land, or what dues he ought to have by the year from the shire . . .
So very narrowly did he trace it out that there was not a single hide,
nor a yard of land, nay moreover not even an ox nor a cow, nor a
swine was there left, that was not set down in his writ. And all the
recorded particulars were afterwartds brought to the King.

*Anglo-Saxon Chronicles*
Information Gathering for the Domesday Book (1086)

Y the middle of the seventh century – although few if
any may have been aware of the fact – the people of
Wigan were subjects of the King of Northumbria.
Northumbria, once the most powerful of the Anglo-
Saxon kingdoms, had been formed by the coming
together of the two kingdoms of Bernicia and Deira,
and had gradually extended its influence – once limited to east of the
Pennines – over the whole area covered by present-day Lancashire,
Cheshire and Cumbria. As far as the people of Wigan were concerned,
their allegiance probably stretched no further than the lord of the
manor in which they lived. Indeed, given the problems of transport
and communication, they would hardly be more aware of the existence
of Manchester than they were of Northumbria!

These were unsettled years – years in which several major Danish
invasions, from the 790s onwards, brought turbulence and bloodshed
on a scale not seen before. However, then, as on many other occasions,
the relative remoteness of Lancashire proved an advantage. While the
Danes – invading first along the coast we now know as Dorset, and
later along the coast of East Anglia – swept much before them as they
moved north, the sting had gone out of their advance by the time they
reached north Cheshire and Manchester. They stopped a few miles
south of Wigan and, in the years which brought the ninth century to a
close, their move was back south rather than on northwards.

The beginning of the following century saw a new invasion – this
time along the Lancashire coast. The Norse 'invasion' was not so much
a military incursion into northern England, but more of a large influx
of settlers. Their approach appears to have been relatively peaceful,

and their intention to seek new homes, new lands to farm and new settlements to establish.

While the majority of the Norse settlements were along the coastal plains, they did move inland and often settled on land which had been ignored by the Anglo-Saxons. The Norse and the Anglo-Saxons appear to have lived in a spirit of cautious coexistence, often with towns and villages close to each other, albeit apparently separate. Records show that the Norsemen did not settle in Wigan, but established their own village at Scholes, on the other side of the River Douglas, and at Skelmersdale.

The Norse settlers were Christians, as by this time were the native Wiganers, so at least religious conflicts were, for a time at least, things of the past. Other struggles were taking place, however, and by the middle of the tenth century, the borders of the Kingdoms of Mercia and Northumbria had been redrawn – with the area of South Lancashire being added to the Kingdom of Mercia, under the rule of King Athelstan. For the best part of fifty years thereafter, relative peace was maintained.

Athelstan never formally incorporated Lancashire into the Kingdom of Mercia, but retained it as a royal property – a little private kingdom within a kingdom. Within that area, the land had been divided into six baronies or 'wapentakes' – Walintune (Warrington), Derbei (Derby), Salford, Blacheburn (Blackburn), Lailand (Leyland) and Neweton (Newton). Wigan lay within Newton Wapentake, and there is believed to have been a royal or baronial manor at Newton itself. In the other wapentakes, the royal manors were at Warrington, Derby, Salford and another at Radcliffe, Blackburn – with others at Burnley, Clitheroe, and Leyland.

At this point, it is perhaps worthwhile to inject a note or two of conjecture as to the size and relative importance of the town we now call Wigan. Much has been written in the past of its importance through the period following the departure of the Romans, the invasions of the Angles, Danes and others, and much of that claimed importance has hinged on the supposition that Wigan was a large, indeed fortified, town. However, it is clear that there is no surviving evidence either to support or reject that proposition convincingly. Indeed, the apparent lack of any mention of Wigan whatsoever in Anglo-Saxon records may well be a significant pointer to the importance of the town.

The lack of any substantial archaeological evidence can be explained – just as with the Roman fort – by the wholesale reconstruction of the town in the nineteenth century. And in any case, as the Anglo-Saxon town would in all probability have been built of wood and thatch, remains of buildings would never be expected to have survived fifteen centuries.

What, perhaps more than anything else, points towards Wigan being a very much smaller town – maybe even no more than a village – in the centuries before the Conquest, is the total absence of a mention of the town by name in the Domesday Book. Surely, if Wigan had been a major economic centre in pre-Conquest south Lancashire, the town's name would have been used for the administrative district in which it lay. No, Wigan's importance in history was to be acted out in later

*Celtic Cross. This ancient cross was set into a wall inside Wigan Parish Church at the time of the nineteenth-century rebuilding. It is one of a number of ancient stones thus preserved. Its history is unknown, as is its date.*

centuries.

The Normans' arrival in England is perhaps one of the most written about, and best-known periods in English history. The former royal lands of north Mercia were all given to one Roger de Poitou by William the Conqueror about the year 1072 or 1073, in appreciation of his loyalty during and immediately after the invasion. Whether or not the people of Wigan knew they had a new master is not recorded. Poitou in his turn divided his new estates up, roughly along the lines and boundaries of the Norse wapentakes, and installed his most fervent supporters as tenant lords of the manors.

In the case of the Barony of Newton, one Warinus Banastre was the favoured follower and, upon payment of a tithe to Poitou – and with the promise of military service should his master Baron require – Banastre became the Baron of Newton and, as such, the lord of the lands which included Wigan. As the division of the lands drew down to smaller units, the Wiganers would no doubt become aware of a change in the wind, and perhaps even knew of their new lord, but the scale of change which was sweeping England as a whole must have escaped them almost completely.

Perhaps the first real appreciation of the new order of things came about as a result of the decision, twenty years after the invasion, to hold the first national census. It is perhaps a reflection of the degree of security felt by the invaders that only twenty years after first setting foot on English soil, they felt confident enough to take on the mammoth task of compiling a complete account of the state of the kingdom in 1086. The information gathering exercise which led to the production of the Domesday Book was a massive undertaking by any standard and, as the first attempt to do anything on such a grand scale, the problems must have been enormous. It was also organised and carried out very quickly. The project was first discussed at the Norman Court in late 1085, and the survey completed during 1086.

Groups of royal officers known as 'legati' were sent to every county in the land with instructions to hold courts of session at which representatives of each town or area would present a summary of the required information relating to their area. Therein lies the root of the sparse information the survey revealed about Wigan – Lancashire as a county did not exist. The baronies of present-day Lancashire – wapentakes in Norse language but 'hundreds' in Norman parlance – were included, for the sake of convenience, in the surveys of Cheshire and Yorkshire, occupying about a page and a half in each of the final two volumes of the Domesday Book.

Perhaps the first problem that the local witnesses had to cope with was one of language. Around the Wigan area the commonly spoken language would have been a mixture of early English with a smattering of Norse – the written language of Norman officialdom was Latin!

The juries that heard the evidence were made up of twelve men for each county – half of them Normans and the other half native English. What appeared in the final volumes was a severely edited summary of the information they heard – a fact which can be proved by comparison between some surviving original transcripts of the hearings for some of the southern counties and the records in the Domesday volumes themselves.

In all, seventeen hundred pages of information resulted from the survey. Every detail of the ownership of land and buildings, the use to which that property was put, the number of mills, the number of workers on each estate and property, was recorded. Most important among the questions, however, were those which related to the value of land and property – as a means of establishing future tax assessment! Also for that reason, questions relating to land ownership and value were retrospective. The present owners of lands were asked its current value, its value in 1066 at the time of the Conquest, and its value before the Norman invasion – just to make sure that the royal rights to taxes and dues had not suffered as a result of the confusion following the invasion.

As a part of Newton, Wigan is not mentioned. Indeed Newton itself only gets a few lines. The value of the entire area – about the same size but not the same shape as today's metropolitan borough – was recorded in the Domesday Book at ten pounds and ten shillings, making it the poorest by far of the six subdivisions of the old royal lands. The Blackburn Hundred, by way of a comparison, was valued at almost three times as much.

David Sinclair, writing in his nineteenth-century *History of Wigan* claimed that the absence of any reference to the town was due to a feud between the King and Roger de Poitou. This is inaccurate on a number of counts. Firstly, Poitou as the baron of all six wapentakes after 1066 would have had little interest in Wigan particularly. Secondly, no petty feud would have been allowed to disrupt the first serious attempt to identify the character and content of the country. There does, however, seem to have been a problem between Poitou and his King, as by 1086 the King himself had assumed control of the area again, and Poitou was clearly out of favour. With the monarch holding the lands around Wigan, there would be even less likelihood of the town being excluded had its importance warranted a mention in the Domesday survey.

Poitou remained out of favour during the remainder of William's reign but long after the Domesday Book and under the reign of William Rufus he returned to royal favour and actually enjoyed further grants of lands from the new King. Based at Lancaster, Poitou was in many ways responsible for the development of Lancashire as an integrated unit – and his new lands at Furness and Cartmel account for the inclusion of those areas within the boundaries of the developing county. He continued to enjoy the benefits of the lands until early in the twelfth century, when he backed the wrong side and had his lands confiscated again – this time by Henry I.

As the eleventh century drew to a close, the small town of Wigan – perhaps no more than a few wooden and wattle houses around a small stone church – was as yet relatively unimportant. Newton was still the major centre in the area. For much of the twelfth century, and into the thirteenth, the history of the area slipped back into obscurity. The real history of Wigan was not destined to begin until the reign of Henry III.

Surprisingly, in view of its later preoccupation with matters religious, the early religious history of Lancashire in general and Wigan in particular was not particularly prominent. A look at the maps of monastic Britain show Lancashire and Cheshire to be much more secular than, say, Yorkshire. Not for the area west of the

Pennines was there to be the proliferation of monasteries, abbeys, priories, friaries and collegiate churches, that there was on the east. While Yorkshire had dozens of great, powerful and extensive abbeys, Lancashire had only a few – Whalley, Cockersand and Furness being the most important – and the area immediately around Wigan even fewer. The priories of Holland and Burscough were small and relatively poor houses. Wigan had a parish church with, as far as can be ascertained, a single incumbent. At the beginning of the twelfth century, the church and the manor were quite separate – the Banastres as lords of the manor are well documented, while the names of the twelfth-century parish priests are not. At the beginning of the thirteenth century, however, the rector also held the manor of Wigan, giving him a secular power which probably far outweighed his religious authority.

Wigan has long claimed to be Lancashire's oldest borough – a claim based on a seventeenth-century account of a charter of incorporation, now lost, issued by King Henry I in 1100. That charter is believed to have granted to the town a degree of municipal self-determination, while still clearly under the 'rule' of the lord of the manor.

The appearance of a fully-fledged town less than a generation after the Domesday survey would seem on the face of it to indicate a remarkable rate of development. Although Wigan's first 'official' charter makes no reference to the earlier grants, this in no way reduces the significance of the rights given at the beginning of the twelfth century. Many early charters merely confirm, or give legal authority to the *status quo* – in other words, they recognise officially what has been in existence for years. It is not unreasonable, therefore, to accept that Wigan's development during the twelfth century was directed and controlled by a group of local dignitaries made up of merchants, the parish priest and the lord of the manor.

Thus the development of organised 'local' authority in Wigan was predominantly controlled by the laity rather than the religious. That fact was very much in the town's favour, speeding up the development of a civil or civic authority in Wigan decades before many similarly sized towns, and centuries before others.

Just how that civic organisation developed is, sadly, not recorded, and can therefore only be the subject of (yet another) conjecture. That the local priest was of paramount importance in bringing together the interested parties who would ultimately direct Wigan's development cannot be denied. But he was a single man – rather than the group of monastics elsewhere – and his influence therefore, while pivotal, was balanced by others – the merchants, and the other 'barons' and landowners of the area.

The complete transition from a feudal system may well have still been centuries in the future, but by the end of the twelfth century or the beginning of the thirteenth, the status of at least some of the townsfolk of Wigan had changed considerably. At the time of Domesday the lord of the manor called the tune; the people of the town were largely at his beck and call. The lord of the manor owned and controlled the land, and therefore controlled the living which was gained from it. The people of the town were, generally speaking, his dependants, working for their keep – being paid either in cash or in kind – and paying for

# Wigan's Markets

**W**IGAN's first chartered market was held in 1245, and continued for centuries, growing and developing. The original site of the markets and fairs in the medieval town – the slope down from Market Place and the fields beyond – was later built upon, and indeed became the site of the town's new Market Hall in the last century. Today that land is covered by the Galleries and the Marketgate Shopping Centre. The old Market Hall was built in 1877 and added to on several occasions – first with a fish market and then with a fruit and vegetable market. Finally, and least attractively, a group of shops was added to both the Market Street and Marsden Street frontages in place of the covered walkways that originally fringed the building.

In front of the main entrance of the Market, the Market Square was both the site of a large open air market each week, and the obvious setting for any great civic events. In its last years, the square was a car park. Towards the end of its life, the Market Hall was a run-down building that was difficult to modernise and had largely outlived its usefulness. The new hall was opened in 1988 on part of the old Market Square site, and in many ways echoed the appearance and atmosphere of the old. The new Galleries Shopping Centre occupies the site of the old Market Hall, part of the Market Square and a number of adjacent streets.

*Below: The Market Square – looking from Market Street across to Hope Street, Hope Church can be seen at the right of the picture. It was demolished in the 1970s to make way for Barclays Bank – whose building has been in use recently as the site office for the new Galleries development. The row of buildings to the left of the church occupy part of the site of the new Market Hall.*
*Above, right: Fire Engine Rally on the Market Square,*

*1890 – the two horse-drawn appliances in the foreground were Wigan's. The event was the fifteenth Annual Meeting of the Lancashire Fire Brigades Friendly Society. Beyond and to the left of Hope Church are some of the buildings in Mesnes Street which were demolished to make way for the Inner Ring Road.*
*Right, below: Peacock's Bazaar was a familiar site in the old hall – but, alas, not in the new.*

MARKET DAY, WIGAN.

01448

their needs either with cash or with their labours. A circular system existed with a single man as the controller of it. That same lord was, effectively, local judge and jury, and tax collector.

As a local micro-economy developed, however, merchants would have moved into the town – probably as early as the end of the ninth century – independent of the landowners and able to determine the progress of their own lives. Those men would have had no immediate allegiance to anyone other than themselves. Their relationship with the land and property owners of the area would have been no more than the legal relationship between owner and leaseholder. With the passage of generations, even that relationship must have become blurred, as rights enjoyed became rights assumed, irrespective of their legal status.

There is ample evidence that merchants throughout England had organised themselves into fraternities or guilds to protect their own interests as early as the end of the tenth century. Indeed, in some advanced communities along the south coast, organised guilds, albeit more religious than commercial, are believed to have been established early in the Anglo-Saxon period.

It is not unreasonable to attribute the formation of local merchant guilds in Wigan to the late-eleventh century, and to project from that starting point that by the beginning of the twelfth century such guilds would have assumed significant influence within the town. Certainly during the reign of King John – 1199-1216 – there is ample evidence that merchant guilds had spread rapidly throughout England, with the establishment of this sort of grouping taking place predominantly in the townships which were moving towards establishing their own civic organisation. Wigan was clearly one of a group of towns pre-eminent in this sort of development.

The merchant guild existed, primarily, not for the good of the town but for the good and protection of its members. Quite often the two roles were entirely compatible, but at other times they were not. The guild offered a measure of protection for the merchants – the group helping, protecting or otherwise supporting the individual. The guild also established rules of practice and these, over a period of time, acquired the mantle of legal respectability. Thus, by the dawning of the thirteenth century, while the lord of the manor remained the ultimate local arbiter on legal matters, the laws recognised and respected by the merchants had an almost equal status.

It is not unreasonable, therefore, to see a situation develop in which the baron, lord or magistrate, and the merchants or freemen of the town worked together in the civic interest. That was the situation which obtained in the early years of the thirteenth century, and which immediately predated the granting of Wigan's first charter.

In Wigan's terms, everything developed from a charter of King Henry III, issued in August 1246. The original is, of course, in Latin, with a few Anglo-Saxon and Norse words which did not readily stand translation:

*Henry, by the Grace of God, King of England, Lord of Ireland, Duke of Normandy, Aquitaine and Count of Angers; to all archbishops, bishops, abbots, priors, earls, barons, justices, sheriffs, chief ministers, and bailiffs, and his faithful subjects greeting; Know ye that we have granted, and by this, our charter confirmed for us and our heirs to our beloved and faithful, John Mansel, parson of the Church of Wigan, that his lands at Wygayun may be a borough for ever, and that the burgesses of the same borough may have a Guild Merchant, with a treasury and other liberties and free customs to that Guild belonging, and that no one who is not of that Guild, may make any merchandise in the aforesaid borough, unless by the will of the same burgesses. We have also granted to the same burgesses and their heirs that they may have rights of local jurisdiction, admission, and attachment within the said borough, and that they may come and go freely, and be free throughout our whole land, and through all the ports of the sea, from toll, custom, passage, pontage, and stallage, and that no Counties or Wapentakes shall have any influence on the tenures which they hold within the borough aforesaid. We have also granted to the same burgesses and their heirs, that whatsoever traders shall come to the borough aforesaid with their merchandise, of whatsoever place they shall be, foreigners, or others, who shall be of our peace, or of our leave, shall come into our land, may come safely and securely to the aforesaid borough with their merchandise, and safely there may stay and safely from thence may return by doing there the right and due customs; we do also prohibit that no one may do injury or damage, or molestation, unto the aforesaid burgesses, upon forfeiture of £10. Wherefore we do will and firmly command for us and our heirs that the aforesaid manor of Wigan be a borough for ever, and that the aforesaid burgesses may have the aforesaid Guild Merchant, with an entry fee and with the other liberties and free customs to that Guild belonging, and that they may have all other liberties and free customs and quittances as is aforesaid.*

*Witnesses hereto:– Richard Earl of Cornwall, our brother, Roger le Pygot, Earl of Norfolk, Peter de Saband, William de Ferrers, Ralph Fit Nichol, William de Cantilupo, John de Plesset, Paul Peyner, Robert de Mustengros, Bartholemy Peche and others. Given by our hand at Woodstock, the 26th day of August, in the 30th year of our reign.*

The rights thus given to the merchants were significant. In addition to become effectively the law makers within the town, they were given individual rights as merchants which were of considerable importance. The right of stallage, for instance, permitted the merchants to set up stalls, without charge, in any markets in the land. Such freedoms of individual action were far removed from the accepted forms of the feudal system which had been in operation for so long. Such freedoms, however, were for the few rather than the many. The merchants represented but a tiny fraction of the population of the town. For the others, the vast majority of the population, subservience to the lord of the manor – in this case Roger de Mansel – still remained. Mansel, however, was probably rarely in Wigan, so the real power lay with the burgesses created by the 1246 charter. As the charter states, Mansel was a close friend of the King, and enjoyed a considerable degree of royal patronage and favour.

By the thirteenth century, the concept of the 'craftsman' was gaining popularity, and in any town which had a significant local industry the merchant guilds were considered less than satisfactory in representing the interests of individual groups of craftsmen. The craft guild – representing the interests of the craftsmen rather than the merchants – began to appear. In Wigan's case craft guilds never assumed significant importance within the borough but in a few cases the idea of the merchant-craftsman did. The broad-based merchant guild, for example, did not apparently satisfy the needs and demands of the tailors, and a Merchant Taylors' Guild was established, and survived into the eighteenth century. Just how many other break-away groups there were, or how many sub-groups of the Merchant Guild were established, is unknown, but there may well have been several.

Perhaps recognising the inevitability of a degree of civic autonomy, Mansel issued the first parish charter shortly after Henry issued his. In it the rights ordained by the monarch were confirmed, but the cleric-baron went further and assigned to the newly created burgesses a long list of rights and freedoms which went beyond those granted by the King.

> *To all sons of Holy Mother Church to whom this present writing may come, John Mansel, Parson of the Church of Wigan, greetings in the Lord. Be it known to all men that I have given and conceded, and by this, my present charter, have confirmed, for myself and my successors, to the burgesses of Wigan, and their heirs and their assigns, that they should have their free town and all rights, customs and liberties, as are contained in the charter of liberty and acquaintance of the Lord King . . . and his heirs or assigns, and that they should grind at my mill, to the extent of twenty measures without payment; and that they should have in my woods sufficient for building and burning, together with the freedom of grazing for the nourishment of their own pigs within my woods, to have and to hold of me and my successors to themselves, and their heirs or assigns, freely and quietly, and honourably, with common pasture, and with all other easements belonging to the said town of Wigan, within the town and without . . . paying annually to me or my successors . . . upon each burgage, twelve pence, at the four terms, viz, at the Feast of St. John the Baptist, threepence, at the Feast of St. Michael the Archangel, threepence, at the Nativity of Our Lord, threepence, and at Easter, threepence, for all secular services, exactions and demands. And I, the aforesaid John Mansel, Rector of the Church of Wigan, and my successors, will warrant all the above written to the said burgesses of the town of Wigan, and their heirs and assigns, against all men and women, forever.*
>
> *John Mansel*
> *First Parish Charter (c.1247)*

In return for an annual rent of twelve pence – payable in four quarterly instalments – the burgesses were given effective self-determination within the town. Each was given five roods of land – about one and a quarter acres – together with the guarantee that it could be passed on to their heirs or nominees. Rights of common pasture, rights to cut timber for construction and for fuel, and the right to grind a quantity of corn without further charge at the mills on the Douglas were also granted.

The town at this time was probably no more than a few dozen houses grouped around the streets near the church. Of these, the oldest are almost certainly today's Wallgate (Wellgate?), Hallgate which led to the manorial hall, Standishgate, and Millgate which led down to the Douglas and to the watermills – owned by de Mansel – which were central to the survival of any agricultural area.

The suffix 'gate' in these names comes from the Norse word meaning 'street' and in no way relates to gates as we know them today. Wigan was not a walled town and did not have gates; suggestions that Wallgate referred to the walls of a fortified town are mere fancy. Other possible derivations for the name have included a corruption of 'Warringtongate', but 'Wellgate' is the more likely. At their junction, the Market Place served both as a trading place for the townspeople

*Edward II's Charter to the Borough of Wigan, dating from 1314.*

and for those from the land tenancies in the surrounding countryside.

It would have been in the Market Place, and in the manner in which business was conducted there, that the new burgesses of the borough would have had their greatest influence. Under that influence, the commercial importance of the town – and the town itself – grew steadily.

The 105 years which followed the granting of Wigan's first charter, five subsequent charters were issued – one each by Henry III, Edward I and Edward II, and two by Edward III. In each case the new charter incorporated the wording of the previous ones, each new monarch confirming his acceptance of the earlier document, and sometimes adding a little bit more by way of civic freedom of action.

The fourth charter – given by Edward II in June 1314 – confirms the Kings's acceptance of the freedoms granted in the first charter, and recognises Robert de Clyderhou as Parson of Wigan. It adds nothing else to the freedoms enjoyed by the priest and burgesses and, given the perpetual binding nature of Henry III's original document, seems legally unnecessary. Perhaps, in a turbulent age, it was felt to be necessary to reassure the burgesses that their hard-won freedoms were not being eroded. It survives in the Record Office at Leigh.

The borough as originally delineated was a small and relatively sparsely populated area for much of the early period. It would appear

that the burgesses of Wigan effectively barred entry to their town to the migrant workers of the day. Whilst their employment was essential to the growth and well-being of the town, their presence within the borough boundaries was not! The River Douglas formed a divide between the freemen of the borough, and the bonded and migrant workers on the other side. For them, a development of the old Danish settlement at Scholes was the nearest they could get to Wigan. Scholes seems to have developed into an almost ghetto-like area before emerging as one of the working-class quarters of the enlarged borough in later centuries. With the Douglas only crossable by a ford until the first bridge was built, probably in the fourteenth century, getting to work must have been at times an unpleasant if not difficult ordeal!

*Corn mills were probably first built on the River Douglas before the thirteenth century. This nineteenth-century photograph shows the mill as it was c.1890, with some sixteenth- or seventeenth-century building still evident – suggesting that the mill had developed progressively, and been modernised over a period of several hundred years.*

---

# The parish church

PARALLEL with the development of the borough, the development of the parish church progressed throughout the thirteenth century.

That there has been a church on the site of the present building since the earliest days is beyond dispute. Exact dates, however, are not

*Opposite, top – The stonework of the lower courses of the parish church tower date from the thirteenth century, later stages dating from the fifteenth to nineteenth centuries. The tower's strange position in relation to the rest of the church has posed historians something of a problem – was it, perhaps, once a detached and fortified campanile?*

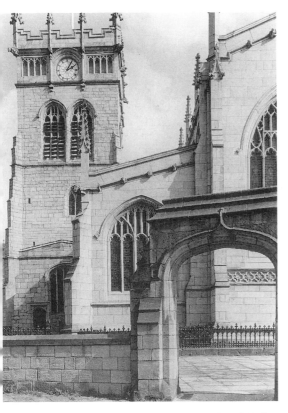

*This medieval font was discovered in the grounds of Wigan Hall, the rector's residence, being used as a means of collecting rain water. It is now to be seen at the west end of the church.*

recorded and the actual sequence of church building which led to the great medieval church of Wigan can only be guessed at. The Anglo-Saxon church may never have been very large. But it was, without doubt, of considerable local importance. Between Winwick in the south and Standish in the north, it was the only church. In those early days, the parish of Wigan, part of York Diocese, was much larger than it is today. Evidence of the Anglo-Saxon church, in the form of anything solid and tangible, probably does exist, but several floor levels below the present one.

The Anglo-Saxon church was, in all probability, the great church of 'Neweton' mentioned at the time of Domesday, as there is no evidence of any other church within the Neweton Hundred. Early in the tenth century, the parish was transferred from the Diocese of York to Lichfield, in which it remained for over four hundred years. The old church, however, was replaced early in the twelfth century with a very much larger building – probably not dissimilar in size and shape to the present church.

Nineteenth-century accounts of the history of the church talk of that Norman building being cruciform in shape, but this is not likely to have been the case. The discovery of the bases of cylindrical columns underneath the columns at the west end of the present nave signify, rather, a large aisled building probably without transepts – the addition of transepts would have produced a church of proportions entirely unlike those normally favoured by the Norman architects and builders.

The construction may well have taken place at the end of the twelfth century and the beginning of the thirteenth, as this would explain the royal appointment of Adam de Freckleton as priest in 1199 – the first recorded priest in the church. The involvement of King John may well have been to celebrate a first appointment to a newly completed – or almost completed – church.

During the century which followed the present tower was either added or rebuilt. (The lower courses of the tower are thirteenth-century in origin, and certainly the oldest part of the building.) Unusually, the tower was built to the north of the church, in the position which would otherwise have been occupied by a north transept. This has given rise to suggestions that the tower was a defensive structure rather than an ecclesiastical one, but again, a lack of records denies us an authentic explanation.

By the close of the thirteenth century, therefore, Wigan was the proud possessor of a large and very grand church. While it occupied the site of the present building, and was about the same size but without the additional aisle chapels, it would have looked very different. In all probability the main body of the church was of Romanesque design, with a short squat tower, unbuttressed, to the north. Entry to the church would have been through a great door in the

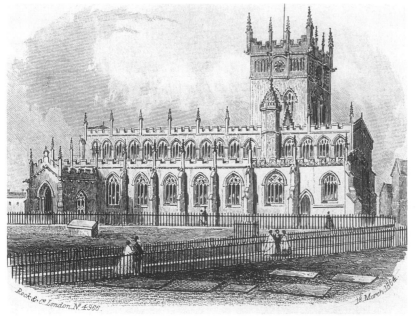

*Early-nineteenth-century drawings and watercolours of the church before the extensive rebuilding later in the century show just how accurate a copy of the medieval original the present building is. Indeed, the present church contains much of the original stonework, redressed and reassembled from the former structure. The representation of so much open space around the church must be put down to artistic licence, as it has been heavily built round at least since the eighteenth century.*

*Thomas Whitehouse, a nineteenth-century liquor merchant, wrote a manuscript history of Wigan, rediscovered earlier this century. He illustrated it with his own hand-coloured drawings, produced between 1826 and 1832; this view of the church comes from that series.*

west gable.

Through much of the thirteenth century, the rectors of Wigan were powerful men of state, and the vicar was the religious leader of the community. Indeed, for much of the period, Wigan's rectors were busy pursuing political careers. The medieval post of rector, therefore, should not be confused with the twentieth-century role. The rectors of twelfth- and thirteenth-century parishes were usually knights and barons – John de Mansel who was rector at the time of Wigan's first

*The interior of the church built between the thirteenth and sixteenth centuries was very elegant – as seen here in a nineteenth-century engraving.*

royal charter is a good example – and held religious sway simply by the fact they they were lords of the manor, owners of all the lands and buildings and, as such, owned the churches themselves. For example, Wigan's first rector, Ranulf, was also Treasurer of Salisbury Cathedral and John de Mansel was one-time Chancellor to King Henry III. Thus, while John de Mansel was instrumental in the granting of Wigan's first charter, it was as a political rather than a religious figure that he did so. While the rectors, as barons, are remembered by history, few vicars – the real parish priests of the community – are thus remembered.

The rectors must be remembered and recognised, however, as the builders of the great parish churches. As local barons, they received all the tithes from the lands under their control, and it was part at least of those tithes which paid for the churches to be built and maintained, albeit using local labour which may not always have been voluntary!

While the burgesses of Wigan were coming to terms with the local responsibilities which came with the town's enhanced status, events were taking place elsewhere which were to develop their roles still further.

In 1265 Simon de Montfort called a national assembly at Lewes – probably the first reasonably representative parliament in English constitutional history. Through the shire knights, and borough mayors where they existed, representatives from the length and breadth of the country were summoned. Wigan, as a borough of some nineteen years standing by that time, ought to have been included, but if it was, all records have been lost. In 1275, a further parliament was called, again seeking representation from all the boroughs. Again, there is no record of Wigan sending burgesses to that gathering.

When it came to the great parliament of 1295, however, records are much clearer. While the two earlier parliaments had been restricted in their membership – to nobility and burgesses – the third great gathering of the representatives of the nation for the first time included the clergy.

King Edward I – often referred to as the 'hammer of the Scots' but who should perhaps be better remembered as a great reformer of English law, politics and constitution – had major military and political problems on his hands. Disputes in France over the ownership of Gascony, recurrent problems with fulfilling his avowed aim to conquer the Scots, and a rebellion in the Welsh hills left him short of both troops and funds with which to wage effective war on three fronts. The steps he took to resolve his difficulties were to lay down the foundations of a parliamentary system which would last for centuries.

Edward decided in 1295 to invoke what has since become known as the 'Model Parliament' – a more universal and representative assembly of the so-called 'three estates' of church, nobility and freemen.

In his summons, the king wrote that

> *What touches all should be approved by all, and it is also clear that common dangers should be met by measures agreed upon in common.*

'All' of course, did not mean 'all' at all! The representatives called may have been truly representative of church and aristocracy, but of the general population, they were certainly not. Like the two parliaments before, the representatives called were selected by burgesses from their own number, and that of course, restricted representation to those few towns – about one hundred and twenty – which did have borough status.

In the royal writ for this model parliament, the king had made much of the democratic process which was to ensue

> *Because we desire to have a conference and treaty with the earls and barons, and other great men of our kingdom, to provide remedies against the dangers the same kingdom is in at this time, therefore we have commanded them, that they be with us at Westminster on the Sunday after the feast of St. Martin, in winter next coming, to treat, ordain and do, so as those dangers may be prevented. We command and firmly enjoin thee that, without delay, thou dost cause to be chosen, and to come to us at the time and place aforesaid, two knights of the counties aforesaid; and of every city, two citiizens; and of every borough, two burgesses, of the most discreet and fit for business; and that the said knights may have sufficient power for themselves and the community of the county aforesaid; and the said citizens and burgesses may have the same power, separately for themselves and the community of the cities and boroughs, then to do in the premises what shall be ordained by the common council, so that for defect of such power, the business aforesaid may not remain undone . . .*

Wigan, as one of the four boroughs of Lancashire, was represented – by William Teinturer and Henry le Bocher – who are reputed to have received a stipend of a florin a day for their services to their King.

The burgesses of Wigan continued to send representatives to Edward's Parliaments until 1306, despite an increasing awareness that their presence had little influence on proceedings. The barons, earls and knights outnumbered the 'commons' and the novelty of sitting beside, and working with the great and the powerful soon wore thin – not just for the Wigan members, but for most if not all the civic representatives present. The stipend they were paid came nowhere near meeting their costs, and the damage done to their businesses, despite the help of their fellow guildsmen, proved too great. In the first quarter of the fourteenth century, more and more boroughs asked to be relieved of the obligation to send members to successive parliaments, and many even sought to pay for the privilege of being officially excused!

In Wigan's case, after 1306 when John Mercer and Simon Payer represented the borough, no member was sent to a parliament for nearly two and a half centuries. From 1307 until 1547 that right – seen as an unwelcome and expensive burden rather than a privilege – remained unused. In many respects, that decision was neither surprising nor ill-conceived. There is evidence from other boroughs of the writ to select members for parliament being overlooked by the crown if past members had shown excessive dissent. There are even instances of borough charters being revoked in apparently persistent cases! However democratic the process may have appeared to be, the power of the monarch was still virtually absolute, and boroughs could be disenfranchised just as easily as they had been franchised in the first place.

Chapter Three

# The medieval town

Moreover . . . we have by this our charter confirmed to the aforesaid
John, and his successors . . . that he and his successors aforesaid, by
their stewards or bailiffs . . . may have power of inquiring as often as
need shall be concerning all excesses, oppressions, extortions,
conspiracies, confederacies, and other transgressions and grievances
whatsoever within the said borough, as well as merchants or others for
the sake of trading and otherwise, we have granted for us and our
heirs to the said John, that he and his successors, parsons of the
church aforesaid and lords of the borough aforesaid, may forever
within the said borough have a certain seal by us to be ordained of two
pieces as is customary to be used for recognition of debts there,
according to the form of the statutes published for merchants . . .

King Edward III, Wigan's sixth charter (1351)

UCH has been written about the establishment of
boroughs in the early Norman period. A number of
Norman boroughs had been established in the years
immediately following the Conquest, but these were
far removed from the status Wigan came to enjoy in
the mid-thirteenth century. The usual type of burgh or
borough established early in the Norman period was a fortified town, a
garrison town. Wigan was not such a borough. Indeed researches over
the years have proved that there were no such boroughs in Lancashire
at all. Thus Wigan was excluded from the requirement to build
perimeter walls, maintain and repair them, and to construct post
defences.

By the beginning of the twelfth century, however, a new definition of
the term was emerging which was much less to do with the need for
self-defence, and more to do with self-regulation. During the twelfth
century the new-style borough status was bestowed by royal charter on
several towns – in Lancashire such grants were made to Preston in
1179 and Lancaster in 1193. Both towns, like Wigan, believe that these
charters were not the first, and that earlier grants had bestowed
effective borough status on both towns during the reign of Henry I. It is
interesting to note that Newton-le-Willows, the one-time centre of the
Newton Wapentake, did not itself achieve borough status until much
later and did not become a parliamentary borough – a status enjoyed
by Wigan since the 1295 Parliament – until 1559.

Borough status was an almost essential prerequisite for any town with its eyes set firmly on a commercial future. As one of the only four boroughs in Lancashire with royal charters, thirteenth-century Wigan was in an important position not just within the emerging county, but also nationally.

Central to the development of Wigan as a commercial centre was the market – held in the Market Place, the focal point of the town. Chartered markets – markets with a legal status – were introduced from the mid-thirteenth century, but there is every reason to recognise the fact that like so many other charters, such grants merely recognised what was already an established practice. Wigan's first market charter was probably issued in 1245, more than twenty years after a similar privilege was granted to Manchester and Salford, and nearly forty years after Liverpool. However, that fact need not influence the very strong proposition that such fairs or markets had been held in the town for a century or more before that date.

If, as has been argued, Wigan had achieved the status of a seigneurial borough – a borough controlled by the lord of the manor rather than burgesses – by 1100, then a market as a means of trading within the borough and with neighbouring communities must have been established within a relatively short period of time thereafter. That the town seems to have developed throughout the twelfth and early-thirteenth centuries around a market place adds strength to that supposition.

As is so often the case in medieval England, commercial and religious activities coincided and overlapped. Many markets were held at the same time as fairs – both being staged to coincide with religious festivals, a practice which continued for centuries. Smaller, purely commercial, markets were a more casual affair but, for the major 'official' events, Church and borough joined forces to create an event which may well have lasted for a week or more, and which attracted merchants and others from near and far. At these major fairs, Wigan's merchants would have welcomed and traded with merchants from boroughs hundreds of miles away. As well as providing trading opportunities, such markets also served a communication role, allowing burgesses and townspeople from opposite ends of the country to meet, discuss affairs of concern and to exchange news.

By the fourteenth century, the weekly or twice-weekly market must have been well established as the focal point of the town's burgeoning commercial activity. The variety of produce and commodities sold in that market directs our attention towards the evolution of the many trades, industries and crafts which were to underpin the expansion and development of the town.

It is interesting to note that at the time of the Domesday survey, the lands around Wigan were not highly thought of by either the Normans or, for that matter, the locals. While other areas of Lancashire and of the Barony of Newton in particular were either being developed or seen as ripe for development as agricultural land, much of the area around Wigan was considered to be empty bogland of little value.

That land, however, was to yield a commodity essential to progress. Peat as a fuel was probably one of the first commodities sold by Wiganers to their fellows and to others outside the town. Peat provided a more efficient source of heat than the wood which had been burned hitherto. It was nothing, however, when compared with coal, and coal is known to have been mined in the Wigan area at least since the fourteenth century. Indeed it may have been mined in the area from a very much earlier date – the word is derived not from a Norman, Danish or Saxon root, but from an early British word predating them all. It is possible, therefore that the use of coal as a fuel was known in Wigan from before the time of the Romans. (There is evidence that the Romans burned coal in some of their stations – but they called it 'carbo' rather than coal.)

Certainly the closeness of the material to the surface, and the ease with which it could be reclaimed in the early days did not require complex equipment or any geological know-how. It was a simple matter of scraping off top soil – perhaps not even that in some cases – and chipping away at the black rock. With cannel coal the most easily mined and the most brilliant when burned, it is even worth suggesting that the material was used as a source of light as well as heat. Of all the cannel coals mined in Britain, even into the present century, Wigan's was the richest and finest, burned the brightest and left the least ash.

So easy was coal to 'mine' in the early centuries of its commercial exploitation in Wigan that there are numerous accounts of one-man activities in the plots of land – and later back yards and gardens – owned or leased by the people of the town. Particularly easy to recover was coal in the centre of the old town, where the seams came very close to, and in places, broke the surface. Stories of the foundations of properties being undermined – literally – by such activities pepper the town's history.

Alongside coal would be the commercial produce of the surrounding lands – the agricultural crops which fed the growing town. With two mills in the town – both on the Douglas – much of that produce would be sold within a production cycle entirely controlled by the lord of the manor and the burgesses – grain, flour, bread and so on, with farmers, millers and bakers central to the town's internal economy.

Equally important by the fourteenth century were textiles, another industry central to the continued well-being and development of the town over the centuries which followed. By the early years of the fourteenth century the industry was sufficiently well established in the town to support three fulling mills – two on the Douglas and one on Clarington Brook.

While the production of cotton was to dominate the textile industry in the nineteenth and twentieth centuries, the early textile industry appears to have been broader based – embracing wool from the sheep of Lancashire and Yorkshire as well as flax and a relatively small amount of cotton imported through Liverpool, or through southern ports.

The actual production of raw lengths of textiles which kept the fulling mills working was, as it would be for centuries to come, a home-based activity. Both spinning and weaving were established trades, albeit still probably secondary to agriculture as the staple industry of the town. Indeed four hundred years would pass before the domestic handloom weaver went out of production.

The three mills were Coppull Mill – at or near the foot of present-day Coppull Lane, the Old Mill of Wigan slightly further downstream, and Lorrington Mill between Wigan and Ince. With two corn mills also being powered by the river, the Douglas was certainly put to good use from an early date!

The fulling mills were probably constructed around the same time that Wigan received its first charter, as fulling stocks, mechanised heavy hammers which did the work previously done by treading the cloth in soapy water and beating it with poles, were introduced into Britain early in the thirteenth century.

The early establishment of a pewter industry in Wigan – another legacy of the Roman period – highlights the town's establishment of trade links with other parts of England – if not also Ireland and the European seaboard – and signals the importance to Wigan merchants of the rights and guarantees of free passage both for themselves and the merchants they traded with which were included in the 1246 charter.

Originally a highly prized material, pewter became a somewhat more utilitarian material – and therefore probably more commercial – after the Council of Westminster outlawed its use for the manufacture of Church vessels in 1175 – taking away at a stroke a market which had existed for centuries. (Once banned from using pewter chalices, many churches buried them with deceased priests, and the burial of such a chalice actually became a custom in many areas!)

However, the development of pewter cups, plates and other vessels for secular use replaced the religious market and pewter remained in use in England for centuries. Some fine examples of the work of Wigan craftsmen in later centuries still survive. Cornwall was the major English source of tin of high enough quality to blend with lead and produce the malleable alloy. Thus Wigan merchants from early times must have established trading links with their Cornish counterparts. The guarantee contained in the royal charters that Wigan merchants could come and go freely, and be free throughout 'our whole land and that other merchants could come safely and securely to the aforesaid borough with their merchandise, and safely there may stay, and safely from thence . . . return' was clearly of paramount importance from the earliest days of the borough.

Pewter remained an important manufacturing industry in the town for centuries. With the manufacture of pewter vessels went a number of associated industries, and the evidence of pewter ware being produced in the town from the thirteenth century at the latest also implies that

*Pottery was an established medieval craft in the town – this animal figure is believed to date from the sixteenth century.*

there was provision for the skills of metal smelting and alloying, smithing, forging and other associated skills also to be available to the craftsman merchants.

To that list of trades already in the town can be added those of ostlers, wagon makers, blacksmiths, tanners, masons and a host of others. Together they brought considerable prosperity and equally considerable improvement to the lot of the Wiganer.

In 1334 an Act in Parliament, requested by the burgesses, authorised the construction of the first bridge over the River Douglas at the bottom of Millgate, linking the town with Scholes and replacing the ford as the normal method of crossing the river, while another of about the same time approved the paving of the main streets to facilitate the passage of wagons as well as horses and people.

A charter of Edward III in 1351 confirmed that the King had granted the borough – through John Winwick the Rector – an official seal for the first time, although a seal believed by many to belong to the seigneurial borough and dating from about 1200 still exists. That seal was, with royal approval, to be used as the official mark on all documents, especially those relating to the regulation of trade in the Market Place and the establishment of debts and dues as a result of that trade. Edward's charter required that custody of the seal would be the responsibility of 'a certain clerk to be deputed by us there'. The 1351 charter confirmed the appointment in the previous year of the town's first Town Clerk.

Edward III's charter states that 'the greater part of the seal aforesaid may remain in the custody of the mayor or keeper of the borough', while 1370 is the date often given as that in which the office of Mayor was officially established. Both offices had in all probability existed unofficially for some time beforehand.

Since the earliest days of borough status, Wigan had had its own 'court leet', chaired by the rector, at which disputes as well as crimes were heard, tried and adjudicated. During the reign of Edward I, such courts had moved from being purely manorial institutions, to being franchised by the Crown, and such an officially franchised court had probably been established in Wigan before the end of the thirteenth century. By the following century, however, great progress had been made towards a system more closely akin to the magistrates' court of today, with a steward who acted as judge, and appointed bailiffs who acted as the executors of the court's will.

In the same 1351 charter which granted the seal, the status of the borough's court was also clarified, giving the burgesses and bailiffs much greater independent scope for action than they had enjoyed previously:

> *no burgess of the said borough or other resident in the same may be pleaded or impleaded before us or our heirs of any justices, sheriffs or ministers of us or our heirs out of the borough aforesaid, concerning lands and tenements which are in that borough, nor concerning transgressions, covenants, contracts or complaints arising in the same borough . . .*

The powers enjoyed by the burgesses were considerable, and equalled by their responsibilities. The concept of a 'local authority' partly self-governing, and partly self-regulating, was by now well established.

While great advances were being made in the commercial and municipal development of the town, the agricultural economy was also developing. Indeed agriculture probably remained the most important 'industry' in the town long after the first borough charter was issued, and perhaps even well into the fourteenth and fifteenth centuries. Agriculture had, after all, a much longer pedigree than commerce. With land – its ownership and its exploitation – being the basis of all local power, landowning families had established themselves in the locality long before the more formal order introduced by the Normans was established. By the time the Normans arrived in England, the Bradshaighs, the Norrises and others were already well established and their influence well known.

What clearly did occur, however, was a temporary displacement of these families as the Normans sought to consolidate their position, power and influence. The Anglo-Saxon families clearly lost their lands to the new Norman barons when the King sought to reward his close friends after the Conquest was satisfactorily completed.

Thus Roger to Poitou (sometimes spelled Poictou in old documents), in acquiring the ownership of the Neweton Hundred, may well have displaced the Bradshaighs and others for a time at least. As this is yet another obscure period of English history, there is no evidence to fall back on. In some cases it seems certain than Anglo-Saxon families were allowed to retain their lands as long as they posed no threat to the Normans, but in other areas Normans assumed control of all the land.

When the Barony of Newton was split up under tenant-barons by Poitou, the Banastres and others – Norman in origin – certainly took effective control. However, by bargaining, or by inter-marriage, many of the old families returned to their old estates either by marriage right or by the purchase of leases. They shared their influence with the likes of John de Mansel, who was without doubt the real power in the area.

The establishment of Wigan Hall – the home of the rector baron – probably dates from the twelfth century and the completion of the new parish church. The use of the name 'hall' as the home of the Rector of Wigan remains to this day. By the end of the thirteenth century, however, the picture had changed considerably. From that time the Standish family's connections with the neighbourhood is well documented. The Gerards, the Woodcocks, the Hollands and the Bankes also appear at about that time and, again, would play significant roles in the coming centuries of Wigan's existence.

There was a hall at Haigh before the end of the thirteenth century, and the fortunes of the Bradshaighs had reverted to their pre-Conquest status. Indeed, from the Bradshaighs comes the one romantic story which no history of Wigan's twenty centuries could afford to be without – the story of Lady Mabel Bradshaigh, which led to the renaming of an ancient cross in the town as 'Mab's Cross'.

The story comes in several versions, and exact dates and circumstances are difficult to ascertain. In some versions, Lady Mabel's plight revolves around the assumed fate of her husband either after the war with the Scots at the end of the thirteenth century, or alternatively at or immediately after the Battle of Bannockburn. In others, it requires him to have been somewhat further afield – during the later Crusades towards the end of the thirteenth century. In yet another version, the

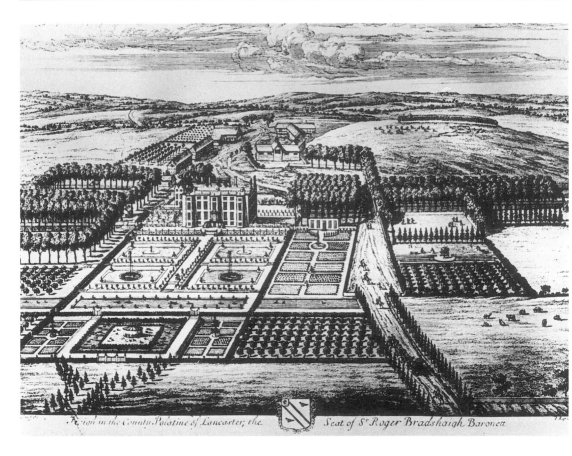

*...gign in the County Palatine of Lancaster; the   Seat of S.ʳ Roger Bradshaigh Baronett*

story is quite fundamentally different – but we shall come to that version in due course.

The different versions of the story fall into two groups – the first perhaps being more fiction than fact, a legend given local interest by the insertion of well-known Wigan names. The second lacks the romantic backcloth, and is much more in keeping with the nature of the times! However, as we are dealing with events of nearly seven centuries ago, either or neither might be true!

The legend of Lady Mabel Bradshaigh impressed both local historians and respected writers. Among them was Sir Walter Scott who deals with the story both in his novel *The Betrothed* and in *Waverley.* Sinclair, in his *History of Wigan,* related that Sir William was away at 'the Scottish Wars', while Sir Walter Scott places him 'ten years away in the Holy Wars'. Scott clearly attributes the story to the time of the Crusades, as the traditional version has Sir William 'dressed as a palmer' when he returned to the town, a form of dress much used by men returning from the Crusades.

Whichever circumstance is correct, the general pattern of the story is the same. After ten years of Sir William's absence, Lady Mabel is believed to have received news of his death. The status of a widow in early-thirteenth-century England was not a particularly secure one, to say the least, and she is believed to have then married a Welsh knight –

*Haigh Hall in its Elizabethan guise, complete with formal gardens. This building replaced the house that Lady Mabel would have known some time in the sixteenth century. Just what the original hall looked like is unknown, but it would certainly have been rather less stately than this noble pile.*

*Mab's Cross. The ancient Wigan Cross was moved to its present position in the 1920s.*

*For centuries it had occupied a site on the opposite side of the road, outside what is today the Mab's Cross Hotel.*

Osmond Neville according to the Bradshaigh version of the story, and Sir Henry Teuther according to that accepted by the Norres family.

But Sir William was not dead. He had been imprisoned for several years but returned to Wigan and to Haigh to reclaim his wife, his family and his estates. The legend tells how Lady Mabel, seeing a man walking in the town, wept when she realised how similar he looked to her late husband. When Bradshaigh revealed himself to Lady Mabel and her new husband, the knight is said to have fled, hotly pursued by the irate Bradshaigh, who ultimately pursued him to Newton-le-Willows and killed him.

Lady Mabel had unwittingly committed the most grievous of sins, and on the advice of her confessor, elected to do penance for the rest of her life. That penance, to be carried out once a week, involved walking barefoot from Haigh to an ancient roadside cross just outside the town, wearing the original penitential sack cloth. There she was to pray for her own soul and the souls of her family. Through all weathers, apparently without remission, Lady Mabel is believed to have carried out her humiliating penance.

Sir William, banished for a year after being found guilty of killing the Welshman, returned to Haigh and his family in due course. His wife's penance, however, continued for the rest of her life. Given that her daily route crossed the Douglas – and there was as yet no bridge, just the ford at the foot of Millgate – it must have been penance indeed throughout the Wigan winters.

Of the origins of the cross, nothing is known. The base, and a stump of the upright, remains on Wigan Lane, in the latest of a number of positions it has occupied over the centuries.

*Lady Mabel and Sir William, as depicted in marble on their altar tomb in Wigan Parish Church. Their bodies are actually buried underneath the church. The altar tomb is no longer complete. The original front and side panels, decorated with scenes from the Mab's Cross legend, are stored in the church out of sight. The original effigy of Sir William was replaced in the last century.*

In the introduction to *The Betrothed*, Sir Walter Scott sets the legend in a much more international framework, showing versions of the same story with origins in Scotland and in Germany – suggesting quite clearly that this is one of those legends which can – and probably has been – applied to a wide variety of locations. In the Scottish version, the wife, left alone in her castle by the banks of the Tweed, has a child which she claims was given to her by a river god who rose up out of the waters. In the German version, the knight's best friend, charged with looking after the lady, is about to marry her the day the knight returns.

An alternative version of the story – which does not involve penance and Mab's Cross – has Sir William described as a less than peaceful landowner who had to flee from Wigan in 1315 after a local feud, and a strong suggestion that he was implicated in a murder. He roamed the country with a group of renegades for several years. He returned to Wigan seven years later, in 1322, after receiving a royal pardon, but there was, in this version of the story, no Welsh knight, no bigamous marriage, and no penance for Lady Mabel.

The Bradshaighs were both buried in Wigan parish church – that much is certain – but they were not buried in the altar tomb, the remains of which can be seen there today. There is no accurate date for that tomb, and that poses an historical problem, as the tomb had carved panels showing Lady Mabel doing her penance, and also Sir William slaying the Welsh knight. Those panels are now stored out of sight and only the effigies remain in the chapel.

Was the tomb contemporary with their deaths – or was it the creation of a later Bradshaigh who had been brought up on the Mab's Cross legend? If the latter is true, then when did Wigan Cross become known as Mab's Cross? Unfortunately, the answers to these questions will never be known.

Lady Mabel, as a descendant of the Norres family, was wealthy in her own right and in 1338, after the death of her husband, founded a

*Sir Walter Scott – the legend of Mab's Cross fascinated him, and he wove it into his novel, The Betrothed.*

family chapel in Wigan parish church, occupying a position in the aisle to the south of the chancel. Endowed with lands from both the Bradshaigh and Norres estates, the chapel had sufficient income to pay the stipend of a vicar to celebrate Mass daily for the good intentions of the family in general, and – if you accept the Mab's Cross legend as true – in atonement for Lady Mabel's unwitting sins in particular. The duty was observed and carried out to the letter until shortly after the Reformation in the sixteenth century.

Today the Crawford Chapel occupies the site, now restored as the Lady chapel in the church, and still contains the Bradshaigh monument with effigies of the unfortunate lady and her husband.

After years of neglect in various parts of the church, the two figures – known locally as 'Adam and Eve' were recognised as the Bradshaighs during the nineteenth-century restoration. The effigy of Lady Mabel is original, having been extensively restored and re-carved in the last century. Sir William was so badly damaged by the time of the restoration that he had to be completely replaced. The original was placed into the monument itself but when that was dismantled in the 1960s it was placed in the chapel where it can still be seen. The original Lady chapel itself became disused after the Reformation, and despite restoration in the seventeenth century, was demolished by the middle of the nineteenth.

Just what sort of conditions these great families lived in, and what quality of lifestyle they enjoyed can only be guessed at. While they were certainly the important figures of their day, the 'Halls' of fourteenth-century Wigan may not have been all that grand. Sadly no trace remains of any of the great houses of the medieval town to cast light on the comforts their residents enjoyed.

It would certainly far outstrip those enjoyed by the simple townspeople. Wigan houses at the time fell into two groups – those of the merchants were often themselves called 'halls', although much less grand than those of their landed neighbours. A merchant might have a house with several rooms – a hall, a larder, a second room downstairs, and a 'solar' or upper room in the eaves above. Merchants' houses had chimneys, while many of their poorer neighbours merely hoped that the smoke from their fires would escape through the thatch! The majority of Wigan houses were described as small and draughty, although they did have windows – some using thin sheets of horn – and later glass – but a few with nothing at all to keep out the winds.

They were probably mostly or all cruck-built – wooden-framed houses with the gaps between the spars of the frame filled either with wattle and daub or with primitive mud or clay bricks, a building style which survived into the seventeenth century.

The manor houses, on the other hand, were usually larger, often stone-built, and very often built around a courtyard. They were often fortified, although by the close of the fourteenth century such precautions were often considered unnecessary except in the more turbulent parts of the country. The site of Haigh Hall – on top of an easily protected rise – suggests that it was probably chosen for safety reasons as well as the view!

Conditions in the town, however, continued to improve with the advance of its commercial importance. The population grew steadily throughout the fourteenth and fifteenth centuries, despite periodic set-backs, as various plagues and diseases, the result of insanitary conditions, took their toll of most English towns. The most famous of them all, the Black Death – bubonic plague – killed over a third of England's population in the fourteenth century.

Suddenly, peasants who had previously worked for their lords out of a requirement of duty, found their services in high demand. Shortage of labourers after the plague meant that crops went unharvested, fields unplanted. Now labour had a price. After the first wave of the plague had subsided, wage rates doubled and trebled, and despite the Statute of Labourers passed in the 1350s in an attempt to restore wage levels and working conditions to their pre-plague level, the lot of the worker had begun to change.

Where previously, work for the lord of the manor had been a requirement in return for the right to till his own land, many peasants now found they could make a better deal for themselves. By the dawning of the fifteenth century, many had managed to change their relationship with the manor to employee rather than bound serf, while others had changed their relationships from peasants to tenants.

In the countryside around Wigan, three distinct groups or classes of people were emerging. The labourer was the employee, albeit now paid for his labours in part at least. The tenant farmer could now direct his own labour, and sell his produce or not as he wished in the market place alongside other merchants and manufacturers in the town. The landowner now had to pay in part at least for the services he enjoyed.

With money spread across a wider group of people, so was taxation. With one exception, each tax or 'fine' was levied according to the capital value involved – the estate owner to the king, the tenant to the landowner and so on – even down to taxes payable upon the acquisition of a sheep or a cow.

The exception was the poll tax levied in 1377. The tax – poll meant 'head' – was levied on every person over the age of fifteen and, although it had been graduated between 1377 and 1379, the difference between the level paid by the aristocracy and that paid by the lowest strata of society was minimal. The 1380 tax, however, levied a standard one shilling per person, irrespective of rank, the exception being beggars. What was an irritation to the rich was a crippling burden to the poor. Families declared fewer members, and fewer adult children than they really had, and royal records showed the adult population of England apparently to have dropped by half a million on two years!

Locally, history does not relate the reaction of Wiganers to the tax, but nationally, the outcome was the famous Peasants' Revolt of 1381 led by Wat Tyler.

Chapter Four

# Reformation and Civil War

The Rectory of Wygan; In the hands of Richard Kyghley. It is worth, in rents and farms, as well as free tenants, as tenants at will in Wigan aforesaid, £25 per annum; also the rent of two water mills, there, £3 6s. 8d. per annum; in corn tithes there £56 13s. 4d. per annum; in hay tithes there 13s. 4d. per annum; tithes of lambs, wool, calves, and flax, annually estimated at £3 16s. 8d; oblations, with other small tithes and tolls, £18 per annum; perquisites, together with market tolls, estimated in common years at £3 6s. 8d. per annum; total value £110 16s. 8d.

From thence there have to be deducted the fee of Robert Langeton, Chief Steward of Wygan £4 per annum, also the fee of Robert Hatton, Bailiff of Wygan, £4 per annum; also the fee of William Walton, under-Steward and Clerk of the Court, £1 6s. 8d. per annum; also the annual pension due to the Cathedral Church at Lichfield, in the County of Stafford, £20; also pence annually due to the Archdeacon of Chester for synods and procurations, 16s. 8d; total amount of deductions, £30 3s. 4d; and there remains thereon a clear £80 13s. 4d; the tithe thereof is £8 1s. 4d.

*Valor Ecclesiasticus*
Valuation of Wigan parish church as required by Henry VIII (1534)

 HERE must have been a degree of local involvement in the fifteenth-century civil war which became known as the Wars of the Roses, but apart from an old rhyme which claims to relate how Richard III's banner was stolen and brought to Wigan parish church, there is little recorded. The war between the Lancastrian and Yorkist factions was decided – but not ended, in 1485 at the Battle of Bosworth, at which Richard III was killed and Henry VII was crowned king by Lord Stanley. The first Tudor king had a relatively weak claim to the throne – descending from an illegitimate half-brother of Henry IV. In return for his services, Stanley was created the first Earl of Derby and endowed with vast tracts of land in south west Lancashire.

In the early years of the sixteenth century, Thomas Linacre, a physician of some renown, became Rector of Wigan – and also served for a time as the king's personal doctor – both to Henry VII and Henry VIII. His surname, of course, lives on in the town to this day.

The English Reformation brought about a fundamental change in the nature of English society, and started the country on a road towards one of the most turbulent periods of its history. That change was less fundamental in a town like Wigan which had grown up without dependence on a priory or an abbey, and which was in any case remote from the capital and the centre of the political and religious debates. The effects of those changes, however, were still felt in many other respects.

In the space of under four years – from 1536 to 1540, the monastic system was almost totally dismantled, removing a network of land control and management which in a variety of forms had existed for a thousand years. It seems that the orders of monks and canons – the Cistercian monks of Upholland and the Augustinian Canons at Burscough for example – disappeared completely from the scene.

Relatively speaking, these local priories were very small. The great abbeys elsewhere in the country were major landowners, and while the local priories did own significant tracts of land, much of the agricultural land around Wigan was already in the hands of secular barons and knights – the families who would evolve into the landed gentry of later years.

Burscough Priory had been founded in the late-twelfth century, but Upholland was a relatively late arrival on the scene and dated only from the mid-fourteenth century.

*Above – Upholland Priory Church – all that remains of the Benedictine Priory which was suppressed by the Act of Dissolution of 1536.*

Both, as small houses with annual incomes of less than £200, were dissolved as a result of the 1536 Act. Monastic buildings were systematically dismantled, except where the church continued to serve a parochial purpose – as in the case of Upholland. Before the end of the fifteenth century, many small monastic houses elsewhere in the country had already been aban-doned, and their wealth and income put to more useful, secular purposes – the endowment of schools, hospitals and so on.

As far as parish churches and their clergy were concerned, the transition from Catholic Church to English Church was a more gentle and less traumatic experience. In Wigan, for example, records show that Mass was still being said for the Bradshaigh family in 1548 – the year in which an Act of Parliament dissolved all chantries and chantry chapels and a year after Henry VIII's death.

Wigan's parish church, by this time much altered and rebuilt from the fourteenth-century structure, and embodying just about every phase of Gothic architecture, came through the Reformation unscathed, and, indeed, may have experienced little, if any change in the incumbents, the services, or the organisation of the parish.

Edward's death in 1553 and his succession by Queen Mary – 'Bloody Mary' as she has become known – certainly placed Catholic rectors back in charge of the parish, had they ever left. Mary repealed all the religious laws which had been passed by Henry and Edward, made her

*Top, right – Pewter was an early and important industry in the town from the fourteenth until the eighteenth century. Pewter plate c.1670 by Robert Bancks and pewter quart measure with lid by William Bancks, 1670.*

*Right – Henry VIII's Town Hall was demolished in the eighteenth century, but featured in the town's seal until the early years of this century. This version of it can be seen high above the main door of the new Town Hall in Library Street.*

peace with Rome and declared England a Catholic country once again. She imposed her new pro-Catholic laws without mercy, and gave the Protestant Church its first martyrs.

Richard Gerrard, proposed by Lord Derby, became Rector in the following year, 1554, and he was followed in August 1558 by Thomas Stanley, a member of Lord Derby's family. Stanley may never have lived in the Hall, as he was at that time also Bishop of Sodor and Man.

Mary died two months later – in November 1558 – to be succeeded by Queen Elizabeth I who attempted, for a time at least, to allow the two interpretations of Christianity to co-exist peacefully. She re-enacted Henry's laws on the supremacy of the monarch in religious terms, but although the death penalty was the required sentence for refusing to swear to the Act, few Catholics suffered fines of more than a shilling for refusing to attend Protestant services.

Most clergy took the oath required by the Act of Supremacy during the early years of Elizabeth's reign – with perhaps only one or two per cent being removed from their parishes for refusing so to do. The Queen restored many of the schools which had been closed by Edward VI, and the sixteenth century drew to a close with great strides being taken in the education of at least the fortunate layers of society.

Wigan Grammar School almost certainly owed its foundation to Elizabeth's reign, but just when is uncertain, as no foundation documents survive. Given that towns of similar size acquired schools of similar status before the end of the century, a date might be guessed at of some time in the 1580s or 1590s. It was certainly in existence by 1597, when a document was drawn up confirming a grant of lands to the school and detailing the scale of the land grants and endowments being made. It might be safe to assume that the foundation was relatively new. By 1616, a group of local dignitaries – merchants and landowners, including the Bankes family and others – were actively

involved in raising the cost of constructing the first custom-built school buildings, and this might support the idea that the school was recently founded and still was housed in temporary buildings within the town.

It was not just a new school which was being established in the town in the sixteenth century. Haigh Hall – the original Norman building – was enlarged and in part replaced with an Elizabethan hall to the most modern design. A considerable amount of rebuilding was also going on both in housing and in commercial property.

During the long reign of Queen Elizabeth, a considerable measure of prosperity had come to the whole country. Trade was buoyant and, supported by a strong navy, England was trading across much of the known world. Indeed, during the century as a whole, despite the social and religious turmoil which was endured, prosperity progressed – hand in hand with a consolidation

of local government.

The 'new' town hall – represented accurately or inaccurately on the old County Borough seal and coat of arms which was in use until local government reorganisation in 1974 – is believed to have been built between the closing years of Henry VIII's reign and the early years of Elizabeth's.

*As late as the nineteenth century, late-sixteenth-century buildings still survived in the town. This old building in Chapel Lane, used as a rag shop, was demolished about 1900.*

Wigan had probably increased in size by about thirty per cent during the sixteenth century – giving it a population of about 4,000 by the end of Elizabeth's reign. With the commercial and industrial activity of the town also growing, there would have been no shortage of work. The wool trade – a staple industry of the town since the earliest times – had developed considerably, with woollen cloths and woollen garments being made in Wigan and exported through both Liverpool and the southern ports. The town had also developed a reputation for clock-making, and supported a thriving industry.

The pleas of poverty which had caused the borough to decline to send delegates to Parliament for over two centuries had ceased to be heard in 1547, when Alexander Barlow and Gilbert Gerard had attended the first Parliament of the reign of Edward VI. Barlow in fact represented Wigan from 1547 until the end of 1555.

Through successive Parliaments of Edward, Queen Mary and Queen Elizabeth, Wigan had maintained its obligation to send two

CHURCH GATES, MARKET PLACE.    J.COOPER WIGAN.

*Sixteenth-century timber-framed buildings lined the narrow alley known as Church Gates until the close of the last century. Medieval Wigan must have looked much like this – overhanging upper floors, narrow streets and alleys. When local professional photographer John Cooper took this picture in about 1895, such buildings had almost all disappeared.*

members, the last of Elizabeth's reign being John (later Sir John) Poultenay and Roger Downes. Poultenay also served in the first Parliament of the new Jacobean era – the longest-serving Parliament of English history to date – which sat intermittantly from 1603, the year of the Union of the Crowns, until 1610.

The Elizabethan era ended with an uneasy religious peace in the country. In large parts of Lancashire, especially in the west, the Reformation seemingly had little effect. In contrast with most of the rest of England, Catholicism still maintained a powerful hold on the affections of most ordinary people in the palatinate. Trading towns like Manchester and Bolton, with their extensive contacts with merchants and others from the south of England, took to the new religion keenly enough, but throughout huge tracts of the rest of the county, most people saw little reason to disavow the religion of their ancestors.

This allegiance continued despite great and increasing opposition and even persecution by the authorities. The Pope was excommunicated, to convert a person to Catholicism became an act of treason, fines for non-attendance at Protestant services were imposed, and the whole state apparatus swung into action against Catholicism at the time of the Spanish Armada, when adherence to the old faith was (unfairly) equated in the government's eyes with treasonable intent.

Yet the old religion survived. Indeed, in parts of Lancashire – Wigan, Wrightington, Parbold and elsewhere – many of the local families staunchly held on to their beliefs. There was even a period during Elizabeth's reign when the recorded number of Catholics actually increased. There was even a small group of Jesuits living and working within the borough, despite legislation which outlawed them.

While some familes continued to practise their Catholic faith, however, some of their neighbours were just as fervent in their adoption of the Reformed Church. The Wrightington family, for example, was staunchly Protestant, while the Worthingtons remained Catholic. Within families, too, there was conflict. It is recorded that at one point during Elizabeth's reign, the men of the Dicconson family were members of the Established Church, while their womenfolk remained Catholic!

Wigan even had its fair share of puritans. Although far more conservative in religion than Manchester or Bolton, there were some who felt that the Elizabethan settlement did not go far enough, and who wanted considerably more far-reaching reform in the Church than had been achieved. Some even went as far as leaving the country,

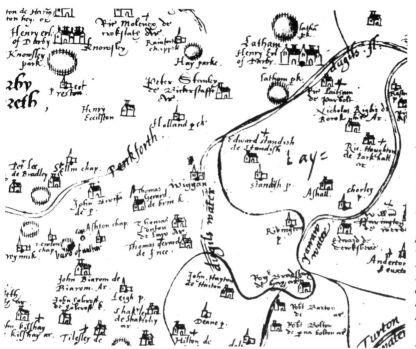

*A section of the earliest reasonably accurate map of Lancashire, drawn up for the benefit of Queen Elizabeth's minister, Lord Burghley, so that he could picture for himself where the known Catholic gentlemen lived. Prominent Catholic families like those of Lord Derby at Lathom, Richard Molyneux of Croxteth and Edward Standish of Standish, can be seen. The River Douglas is marked, as is 'Wiggan'. The map is dated 1577.*

hoping to set up a more ideal kind of society in the New World. Early in the reign of James I the first groups of disillusioned puritans had left England for France and Holland, hoping to find a more sympathetic hearing there than in England. In 1620, they went further, applying for and receiving permission to settle in America. Aboard the *Mayflower*, the Pilgrim Fathers left Europe for a long and uncertain crossing to the New Plymouth colony with, among their number, Captain Miles Standish.

Miles Standish was a member of the great local family, not from the Standish or Chorley branches, but from the Isle of Man. He did, however, inherit some of the local Standish estates, and is the earliest strong link between a local family and the New World. At the age of about sixteen, he appears to have joined Elizabeth's armies as a junior officer, and later is recorded as being part of a military contingent sent to assist the Dutch. Perhaps no more than coincidentally, he was in the Netherlands, and more specifically in Leyden, at the same time as the self-exiled puritans. Many writers, however, take issue over suggestions that he himself was a puritan, suggesting instead that he was merely a salaried officer protecting the Pilgrim Fathers. It is certainly true that he never did join the Pilgrim Church in America – and that is given as the reason for him being denied a colonial governorship – but it is equally probable that he did have puritan leanings, if perhaps not quite so committed to all of the puritan ideals as some of his compatriots.

It seems clear, therefore, that most strands of contemporary religious thought were represented locally, but all the available evidence suggests that the reality of the religious divisions was considerably exaggerated by the time reports of it arrived in London. Most ordinary

*Right – Orlando Bridgeman – one of Wigan's two representatives to Charles I's Parliament in 1640. Bridgeman polled 112 votes – 8 more than his nearest rival.*

Lancastrians lived quite happily together regardless of religious affiliation, at least in normal times.

Times were not always normal, however, and by the 1630s unmistakable tensions were beginning to appear within the country, which were destined to spill over into the unparralleled struggle known as the English Civil Wars. The causes of that great conflict are many and various – Laud's religious innovations and the perceived Catholic inclinations of the court; the financial irregularities and the 'unparliamentary' taxation; the failure to call a Parliament during the whole decade; the imprisonments and the 'forced loans'.

Parliament, indeed, became the focus for much of the discontent that continued to rumble and grow through the reign of Charles I, and parliamentary boroughs like Wigan gained an enhanced role in the political life of the nation. Elections began to be contested, sometimes vigorously, and open factions emerged within the town.

From Charles I's third Parliament, much information comes to us on the method of election within the borough of Wigan. According to the ancient poll records, 138 burgesses were eligible to vote, but only 74 did so. The method was simple. In the town hall, the assembled burgesses were asked in turn to declare the names of their chosen two candidates from a list of those willing to represent the borough. In 1627, seven burgesses stood for election. Sir Anthony St. John polled 65 votes and Edward Bridgeman 63, and both were duly elected. Robert Gardner came third with eight votes and the other four candidates – Edward Boulton, Peter Honiford, William Prescott and Miles Pooly polled just one vote each.

That Parliament sat for one week short of a year, but the outcome of its debate was so unsatisfactory as far as the King was concerned that he neglected to call a Parliament for the following twelve years, ruling by his own authority. When shortage of money and the need to march against a rebellious Scotland forced Charles I to recall Parliament in March 1640, Orlando Bridgeman and Alexander Rigby made the long journey to represent Wigan only to find themselves, three weeks later, on the road north again with Parliament dissolved by the King.

By that time the number of burgesses eligible to vote in Wigan had approached three hundred – with a number of members of the aristocracy added to the list as 'honorary burgesses'. Representation in 1640 had either acquired a novelty value – so long had it been since the last election – or was deemed to be of considerable importance, for almost all the 'official' burgesses exercised their voting rights. Less than a third of the honorary electors did so.

In the elections for the appropriately named 'Short' Parliament, Bridgeman polled 112 votes and Rigby, a leading local Puritan, polled 104. Sir Anthony St. John first elected in 1625 and returned with 65 votes in 1627, this time managed only four votes!

By the end of the year, the King was in even deeper financial trouble, and Parliament was recalled in the autumn of 1640. This became known as the 'Long Parliament' by virtue of the fact that it remained in session, nominally at least, for thirteen years.

It was the first parliament which openly admitted to 'factions' and as the rift between the King and many of the representatives grew deeper, members became more open about their 'royalist' or 'parliamentarian' leanings. Hitherto, Wigan's representatives had been decidedly apolitical, but when the 1640 election returned Rigby and Bridgeman again, it was as parliamentarian and royalist respectively. The election itself provided evidence for the increasing divisions within society, as

*some inferior persons, inhabitants, labourers, and handicraftsmen, being free only to trade with Wigan, and not enrolled or sworn burgesses of the corporation, had combined and confederated and plotted together to disannul and annihilate the election of Bridgeman and Rigby by the burgesses of the corporation.*

The elections were confirmed in the end, although within two years Bridgeman had been expelled for his royalism (he later sat at the King's alternative, royalist parliament at Oxford), and for the next three and a half years Wigan had a single representative.

Despite the presence of Alexander Rigby in the Commons, Wigan came down firmly on the side of the king. The split loyalties within the borough mirrored those of the county and, indeed, the country. At first, the overwhelming desire of ordinary people was to avoid the approaching storm, and many fervent declarations of neutrality were couched in terms of undying support for both sides or, as they diplomatically put it, 'for King *and* Parliament'. Much of Lancashire, including Wigan, was royalist in sympathy; during the first few months of the war all of the castles, all of the arms and ammunition, most of the towns and most of the strategic points in the county had declared for the King; large numbers of royalist forces were levied and were marched off to fight for the King in the south of England. In Lancashire only Manchester held out for the parliamentarians at the beginning of the war, suffering an unsuccessful, week-long siege by Lord Strange (later Lord Derby) for its pains late in 1642.

For the remainder of 1642, however, Derby's army moved through-out the county, causing considerable havoc. They were apparently known as the 'Wigan Cavaliers', and one account recalls the attack on Hindley's puritan church just before Christmas.

In early 1643 the army moved on puritan Bolton (widely known as the 'Geneva of the North'), traversing Rivington Pike, and becoming involved in a series of skirmishes around the outskirts of the town. Several attempts to sack Bolton failed, and the army retired to Lathom House, near Ormskirk, to protect Derby's headquarters. The oppor-tunity for the parliamentarian forces to settle an old score was not to be missed, and Wigan fell to the Roundheads in April 1643. A few stalwarts held out in the parish church tower long after the town had been taken, and the last eighty-six men of the royalist garrison only came down when the parliamentarian commander, Colonel Rosworm,

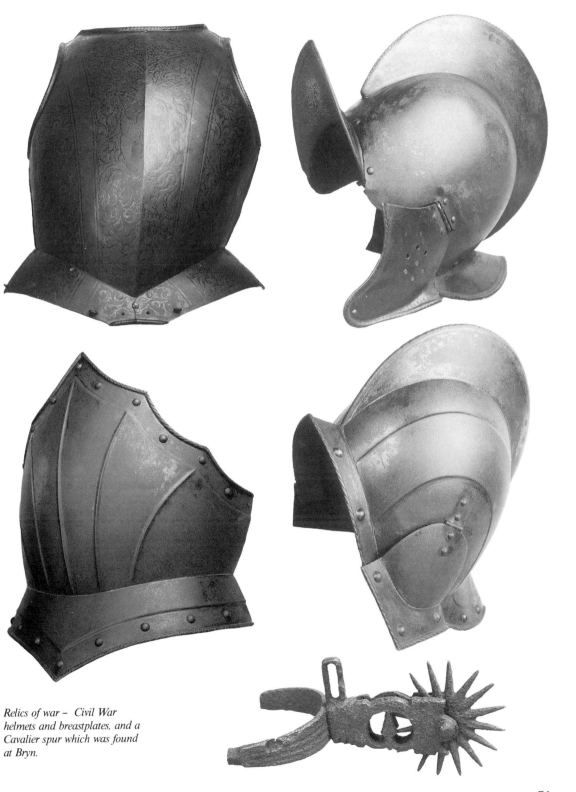

*Relics of war – Civil War helmets and breastplates, and a Cavalier spur which was found at Bryn.*

threatened to destroy the tower and them with it.

Amazingly, considering the royalism of the county as a whole, the parliamentarians had won control of the entire county within a dramatic nine-month period, and by the end of 1643 Lathom House was the only major royalist stronghold holding out in the area; in the following year that was under heavy siege by parliamentarian forces commanded by (now Colonel) Alexander Rigby. Help was close at hand, however, for a major royalist force under the command of Prince Rupert was at that time moving swiftly north. Wigan was recaptured in the late spring of 1644, Bolton was sacked and Liverpool taken, before the victorious royalists headed east into Yorkshire and their fateful confrontation with the parliamentarians at the battle of Marston Moor. Following the royalists' defeat there, much of Lancashire was again re-taken for parliament and even Lathom House succumbed after a renewed siege.

Then, in 1648, the King reached an agreement with the Duke of Hamilton and his party in Scotland that they would lend their support to his cause in return for a guarantee that he would declare presbyterianism to be the established religion of the country. At the head of a Scottish army, he moved south and the Civil War entered its most surprising phase. The Duke led an army of Scottish presbyterians against a combined force of English presbyterians and puritans.

When the King's forces entered Lancashire, Cromwell was in Yorkshire – having assumed that the invasion would come on the east side of the country. He quickly – surprisingly so – crossed the Pennines with his forces and, after a decisive encounter at Preston on August 17, continued his move south. A few days later, his troops were camped near Wigan, from where he continued his move south through Warrington. He was not having it all his own way, however, for his letters tell of battle and march-weary troops – on both sides – and of an uneasy night only three miles from the enemy forces.

> *At last the enemy [the Scots] drew up within three miles of Wigan; and by the time our army was come up, they drew off again and recovered Wigan before we could attempt anything upon them. We lay that night in the field close by the enemy; being very dirty and weary, and having marched twelve miles of such ground as I never rode in all my life [the roads were virtually impassable after a very wet and rainy spell], the day being very wet. We had some skirmishing that night with the enemy near the town; where we took General van Druske and a Colonel, and killed some principal officers, and took a hundred prisoners; where I also received a letter from Duke Hamilton, for a civil usage towards his kinsman Colonel Hamilton whom he left wounded there . . . The townspeople, a great and poor town, and very malignant [i.e. very royalist in sympathy], were plundered to their very skins by them.*

Cromwell's victory was complete, and Charles I's actions in renewing the civil wars by invoking the help of the traditional enemy from north of the border were rewarded by his being tried for treason. Parliament became more and more isolated. John Holcroft, who had replaced Bridgeman as Wigan's second MP in 1646, was apparently purged of his seat, again leaving just Alexander Rigby to represent the town in the now much reduced 'Rump' of the original Long Parliament. The King was executed on 30 January 1649.

In Wigan, despite a law in 1643 which effectively set up local watch committees to purge the clergy and churches of all non-puritan practices, little immediately changed and the Rector, Dr. Bridgeman, remained in office. In 1644, however, all his lands and properties were sequestrated and he was removed from his position, to be replaced in 1645 by James Bradshawe. Five years later Bradshawe, a presbyterian, was himself removed for not being strict enough in the observances now required by the Independents, and Charles Hotham, Wigan's only truly puritan incumbent, took up his post in the parish church.

During the early-1650s, with puritanism firmly in control, persecution of the Catholics began again, with many leading Catholic families having their lands taken away from them and themselves suffering intensified persecution.

Royalism did not die with Charles I, of course, and two years after the King's execution, another Scottish army moved south in the summer of 1651 under Charles IIs banner. Lord Derby, now based on the Isle of Man, was determined to support them. He landed near Glasson in early August and, gathering men as he went, moved south towards Lathom House, arriving there on August 16th. From there he marched via Upholland to Warrington, where he joined up with a cavalry regiment, and turned back northwards through Wigan and on to Preston. At the head of the column with Lord Derby was Major General Sir Thomas Tyldesley, an almost fanatical supporter of the royalist cause. Gathering more men at Preston, Tyldesley turned south again at the head of a small and untrained army of about fifteen hundred men, ill-prepared for what lay ahead of them.

The army spent the night of August 24th near Preston and by lunchtime on the following day had almost covered the eighteen miles to Wigan. His plan was to move on south to join up with the major contingent of royalist forces at Worcester for a combined assault on the strongholds of the Commonwealth. It was not to be, and in a single afternoon the entire direction of the Civil War was altered – about a mile from the centre of Wigan.

Roundhead intelligence had warned of their approach – indeed, every aspect of Derby's move since leaving the Isle of Man had been passed on – and a trap had been laid. At the head of a small army of Roundheads, Colonel Robert Lilburne (MP for the East Riding of Yorkshire and a signatory to Charles I's death warrant) had moved into a strategic position just north of the town and lay in wait for Tyldesley and Derby's army.

In 1651, the town of Wigan probably extended no further out from the centre than Mesnes Street, with the whole of the Standishgate hill and Wigan Lane nothing more than a main road through open country. It is hard to imagine it without today's urban development, but there was probably no building done at all from the edge of the town until a few houses were reached in Coppull Lane, occupied by the families who operated the mills on the Douglas. Beyond Coppull Lane there was only countryside – wooded on one side, with the steep slopes of the hill down to the Douglas on the other. It was in this fine cover that Lilburne's forces waited.

Whether by accident or design, Lilburne's forces revealed themselves to the advancing royalists and battle lines were drawn up by both sides. Seventeenth-century battles were usually set-piece affairs,

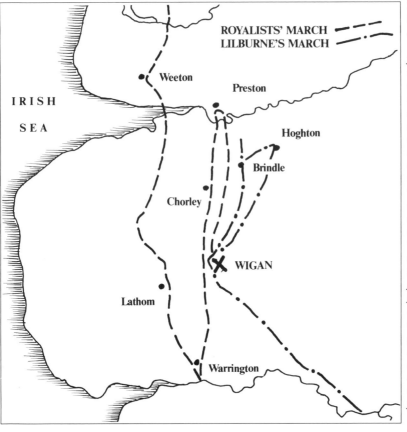

ROYALISTS' MARCH — — —
LILBURNE'S MARCH — · —

IRISH
SEA

Weeton

Preston

Hoghton

Brindle

Chorley

✗ WIGAN

Lathom

Warrington

*The road to Wigan Lane. The royalists landed at Preesall on August 15, then marched to Weeton, near Kirkham, before fording the Ribble and moving on to Lathom the following day. Meanwhile, the parliamentarian Colonel Robert Lilburne had been ordered to Lancashire and reached Wigan on the 21st, hoping to find the royalists there. But they had already moved north to Chorley, and then to Preston, where they stayed for several days. Lilburne, anxious to avoid a fight until his infantry arrived, encamped at Brindle where his battle-hardened troops were caught in a surprise attack which they managed to fight off. Lilburne moved further off to Hoghton on the 24th, still waiting for the reinforcements that were being promised daily. The royalists, knowing, this, decided to wait no longer and marched south. As we have seen the two sides eventually met in Wigan Lane for the final battle of the Civil Wars in Lancashire, and arguably one of the most important.*

*It was here, on the slopes above the river – between the Douglas and Wigan Lane itself – that Lilburne's forces lay in wait for the royalist army.*

and it may well have been intentional on Lilburne's part to make his presence known rather than to exploit the military advantage of an ambush.

They were probably almost equal in number – Derby having a slight advantage – but Lilburne's forces had the advantage of being better trained, better equipped, and certainly of being better prepared. The majority of Derby's men were foot soldiers, augmented by Major General Massey's cavalry. The parliamentarians had the advantage of a larger contingent of cavalry, but fewer men in total.

Derby's major disadvantage was perhaps in the question mark which hung over the degree of commitment and support he could expect from the Scots. Their staunch Calvinist leanings meant they had little time for the Anglican and Catholic contingents in the royalist forces, and were in fact fighting in the probably forlorn hope that the King would – as had once been promised by his father – declare Presbyterianism as the official religion. Having already apparently failed to persuade Derby to change his religious allegiance since joining up with him, there were growing murmurs within the Scottish troops that they were on the wrong side! Just how much these considerations affected the outcome of the battle is unknown, but combined with the lack of military training of over two thirds of the royalist force, Derby and Tyldesley clearly did not have the upper hand. Battle, however, was inevitable.

It did not look promising! The royalists could not contemplate retreat, but knew that their chances of defeating superior forces were at best slim. Undaunted, Derby quickly marshalled his troops and prepared for action. The engagement started in the early afternoon, and, despite heroic actions by many of Derby's troops, they were quickly and steadily pushed back towards Standish.

It has to be said that Derby's military record throughout the Civil Wars was far from convincing, but no one could doubt his personal bravery. Against all odds, he refused to accept defeat and rode back into the thick of the battle, suffering several serious wounds as a result. All around him were the dead and the dying – with heavy losses on both sides. Many of his soldiers fled, leaving the remaining royalist forces outnumbered but quite clearly undaunted. Superior training and superior firepower, however, steadily made the outcome more and more apparent. Almost half of Derby's army lay dead in less than two hours, and over a third were prisoners. Among the dead lay Sir Thomas Tyldesley and Lord Widdrington.

Twenty-eight years later, in 1679, Alexander Rigby would pay for a monument to Tyldesley to be erected on the spot on which he is believed to have been killed. It still stands by the side of Wigan Lane and near Widdrington Road, named after the other eminent casualty of the battle.

Derby and some senior officers fled from the field of battle when all seemed lost, and surprisingly, headed south into the town rather than back northwards to safety. His wounds were tended by a local publican and he eventually made his escape to join the King's armies at Worcester.

The following day, August 26th, Robert Birch, the Roundhead military commander of Liverpool received Lilburne's account of the battle:

*Wigan 25th August 1651*

> *Honoured Sir,*
> *The Lord hath pleased, this day, to appear for us, in the total rout and overthrow of the Lord of Derby and his force, which was increased to about 1,500. He himself, though wounded, escaped, though narrowly. I would only entreat you to send out what horse you have or can get, to ride up and down the country to gather up stragglers. I cannot enlarge myself at present, but entreat you to accept this from him that desires to express himself. Your ammunition is come safe.*
> *The Lord of Derby I hear is fled towards Bolton, but his sumptures and treasure is here. We intended for Manchester this night, and had hopes to take my Lord General's regiment of foot, and to have had five hundred men in readiness to join them. The Lord Widdrington cannot live long. Colonel Boynton and Tyldesley are slain. I have divers other colonels prisoners.*
> *Your very humble servant*
> *Robert Lilburne.*

Surrendering after the Battle of Worcester, Derby was tried and executed for treason – his execution reportedly supervised by Colonel Alexander Rigby, Burgess of Wigan and Member of Parliament for the town. Tradition has it that the scaffold on which he was executed was built of timber taken from the woods around his home at Lathom House. The charges against him had nothing directly to do with the battle, but much to do with his Royalist support. On one count he was charged with breach of a law which forbade anyone from lending support to Charles Stuart. On the other count, he was held responsible for the death of almost one-third of the population of Bolton during the attack on the town by the Royalists in 1644. Derby's body was brought back up north and lay in Wigan overnight before moving on to Lathom House, and on to Ormskirk Church for burial.

Just how extensive had been the damage to the town itself as a result of the skirmishes, sieges and the battle, is not known. The town is often described as 'dismantled', but in seventeenth-century parlance, that could just mean 'stripped of defences'. It could also mean 'roofless', and the true state of affairs may be somewhere in between the two. Certainly damage had been caused to the buildings around the parish church during the siege, but it is unlikely that the town itself suffered as a result of the Battle of Wigan Lane, as the site of the battle was fairly well distant from the town. Indeed, the site has been variously placed at distances of between one and three miles from the parish church – the centre of the town – which could place it anywhere between the Tyldesley monument's present site, and somewhere between Boars Head and the river.

However slight the physical damage caused by the war, the economic and social dislocation was extensive. Wigan was a garrison town for significant periods, with all the costs and burdens involved in the quartering of troops, and the economy of the whole area suffered directly as a result of the war. Things had got so bad by 1649 that the following petition from the Wigan area was delivered. The beauty of the prose cannot hide the reality of the distress:

> *The hand of God is evidently seen stretched out upon the county, chastening it with a three-corded scourge of sword, pestilence and famine, all at once*

*The Tyldesley Monument on Wigan Lane marks the supposed spot where the General fell during the Battle of Wigan Lane.*

*afflicting it. They have borne the heat and burden of a first and second war in an especial manner . . . In this county hath the playe of pestilence been ranging these three years and upwards, occasioned chiefly by the wars. There is a very great scarcity and dearth of all provisions, especially of all sorts of grain, particularly that kind by which that country is most sustained, which is full six-fold the price that of late it hath been. All trade, by which they have been much supported, is utterly decayed; it would melt any good heart to see the numerous swarms of begging poore, and the many families that pine away at home, not having faces [i.e. being too proud] to beg.*

After the dust had settled after the Battle of Wigan Lane, the borough entered a period of relative quiet. The final acts of the Civil War drama were played out elsewhere, and in April 1653, the Rump Parliament finally came to an end and Cromwell assumed total control with a group of advisors. It was not just the Royalist boroughs which were without representation during that first period of Commonwealth rule – Cromwell effectively did away with Parliament for a year. When he did assemble a Parliament in 1654, the boroughs were not represented and until his son Richard Cromwell succeeded him as Protector in 1658, that state of affairs continued.

The 1659 Parliament was called along the lines of the pre-Commonwealth assemblies and Wigan, once again, elected and sent two members to the Commons. Both were puritans – Robert Markland and Hugh Forth.

In 1660, national disillusionment with the Commonwealth finally came to a head and a group of delegates sailed to Holland to meet the exiled King Charles II and invited him to return to England and assume the throne. When elections were held for the new King's first 'Convention' – he did not use the term Parliament – Wigan for some reason returned two quite separate lists of names. On one list, the puritan Forth was returned along with William Gardiner. On the other, the names of John Molyneux and Roger Stoughton were listed. All four appear to have presented themselves at the Commons, but the election was declared void and a second writ issued. This time there was no doubt, and Molyneux and Stoughton, both Anglicans and staunch monarchists, represented the town until the Parliament was dissolved at Christmas.

The campaign was of interest in that, for the first time, the merchants and residents of Wigan seem to have united in an attempt to have their say in the new elections. During the Commonwealth

*A seventeenth-century trading token – worth ½d and issued by Thomas Cooper of Wigan.*

period, where elections had taken place in the country, voting had not been restricted to the burgesses. Other influential figures had been given a vote. Indeed, in Wigan this had been the case long before the Cromwellian period, although the town itself was denied a vote while he was in power. In the Parliaments of Charles I, the electoral role had been increased to over double its original number by the creation of 'honorary burgesses' – merchants and others whose influence within the town was significant. The Parliament called by Richard Cromwell and the first called by King Charles II, however, had reverted to the earlier system of the election of two burgesses by their fellows – effectively disenfranchising some two hundred or so residents of Wigan.

The first Parliament of Charles II had been announced as a 'free' Parliament, and, as a result, many had high hopes for it. This restriction of electoral rights to many people, fewer than had previously been the case, was part of the reason for the emergence of political parties over the next two decades. There were, of course, other reasons – attempts to assert, maintain and develop the role of Parliament, to curb the power of the newly-restored King, and to further religious ambitions amongst them.

During the seventeen years of that Parliament, members who had been elected largely on personality divided into two factions – Whigs and Tories. While the Tories were monarchist, advocates of the Established Church of England and defenders of the newly re-established *status quo*, the Whigs – taking their name from a Scottish presbyterian movement – were dedicated to the assertion and expansion of parliamentary power, and were, initially at least, generally adherents to either the puritan or presbyterian religious creeds. It was by no means an even split, however, and the Commons was predominantly Anglican and monarchist. What puritan voice there was to be heard was a small and muted one. The Parliament passed a long list of pro-Established Church laws, some of them to the dismay of the King. Bishops returned to the Upper House, and the influence and freedom of movement accorded to the nonconformists – presbyterians, puritans and others – was severely limited.

While some towns may have found these laws difficult to live with, Wigan did not. Always a Royalist borough, the people of Wigan were delighted in the return to that which they had always preferred. The Puritan Rector, Charles Hotham was ejected from Church and Hall in 1662, and replaced, on the proposal of Sir Orlando Bridgeman, by George Hall. Bridgeman, ejected from the Commons in 1642, was a man of influence again!

In Parliament, the Earl of Ancrum and Geoffrey Shackerly were returned in 1661 without any political 'labels', but when Ancrum together with Sir Roger Bradshaigh returned to sit in the 1679 Parliament, it was under the Tory banner. Bradshaigh also served as Mayor on three notable occasions – in 1661-2 and again in 1679, the year of his election to Parliament. His final term as Mayor was 1684-5. His son, also Sir Roger Bradshaigh, would serve as member of Parliament for little short of fifty years, from 1698 until his death in 1746, first as a Tory, but later as a Whig. He was also Mayor on four occasions between 1698 and 1729.

The mayor and burgesses of Wigan were not slow in sending their greetings to the King on his restoration to the throne, and in making a plea for the borough's ancient rights to be confirmed and re-established. Charles II agreed, and a lengthy charter re-affirms all the old rights, repeats in condensed form in a preamble the ten previous charters granted to the borough and, at some length, defines the powers, offices and rights of the council.

The charter is dated – as was the usual style at the time – not with a date in normal terms, but by the year being referred to as the fourteenth year of the King's reign. This had led to some confusion over the actual date of the charter, as Charles II had claimed the throne on the death of his father in 1649. In earlier histories the charter is thus dated as 1663, three years after the Restoration. Some later writers have incorrectly attributed the charter to fourteen years after the Restoration – dating the Wigan Charter to 1674. In actual fact, neither date is correct, as the charter is dated not fourteen years after the King came to the throne, but as is stated 'in the fourteenth year of our reign'. We are therefore looking at a charter which was issued without doubt in 1662.

Given that the town appears to have acknowledged its allegiance to the new King fairly swiftly after the Restoration – perhaps in late 1660 or early 1661 – the charter might be expected to have followed relatively quickly. With the date of 1662, then that acknowledgement followed within two years. Such was the enthusiasm with which the King was welcomed to the throne, that the Commonwealth was officially deemed never to have existed!

*Charles II's 1662 Charter was perhaps the most significant in the development of the borough. In the elaborate initial letter which opens the Charter, the King himself is portrayed.*

> *. . . Know ye therefore that we, graciously desiring the improvement of the borough aforesaid, and the prosperous condition of our people there, and revising and taking in good part the many and great services so seasonably bestowed by that borough to our Most Serene Father of blessed memory in the late most calamitous times, and also the continued fidelity and exceeding willing affection of the inhabitants of the same borough towards us and for our service, of our special grace and of our certain knowledge and mere motion have willed, ordained, granted, and confirmed, and by these presents for ourselves, our heirs, and successors do will, ordain, grant and confirm to the aforesaid mayor bailiffs and burgesses of the borough aforesaid, and their successors, the*

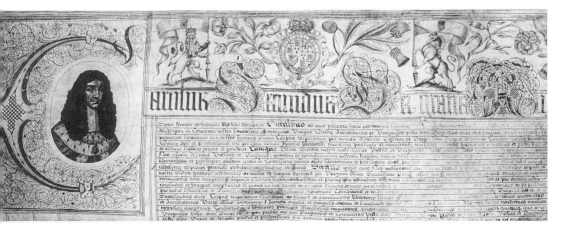

*aforesaid body corporate, and all manner of liberties, free customs, immunities, exemptions, easements and jurisdiction, and hereditments whatsoever which the burgesses of the vill or borough of Wigan aforesaid, or which the burgesses and community of the vill or borough of Wigan aforesaid, or which the mayor, bailiffs and burgesses of the vill or borough of Wigan aforesaid, and their predecessors whomsoever, by whatever names they were rated or called, or by whatsoever name or incorporation or pretence of whatsoever incorporation they have heretofore been incorporated, lawfully had, held, used, or enjoyed . . . by reason or pretence of any charters of letters patent by us or any of our progenitors . . . by these presents in form aforesaid, confirmed in such ample manner and form to all intents and purposes, as in times past they have had, held, used or enjoyed . . . and confirm to our beloved Roger Bradshaigh, Knight, now the mayor of our borough of Wigan aforesaid, to be and continue mayor of that borough for and during the accustomed time of his continuing in that office, according to the use and custom within that borough in that behalf in times past accustomed . . .*

The answer to the precise dating of the charter lies in the reference to 'our beloved Roger Bradshaigh, Knight' and to the exact terminology of the charter. The precise date of the charter is given as May 16th, 'in the fourteenth year of our reign', As Charles was dating his reign from the death of his father, then the fourteenth year was, indeed, 1662. 1649 being the first year.

Wigan has a record of the mayors of the borough dating back to well before the Restoration and, a check of that list reveals that in May 1662, Roger Bradshaigh was reaching the end of his year of office. He was not mayor again until 1679.

While confirming past rights and freedoms, the King's charter also required those wishing to hold civic office to swear to the Oath of Obedience and the Oath of Supremacy. Contained within the charter as well was an extension of the rights of the mayor, burgesses, bailiffs and people of Wigan to own, buy and sell land, subject to a maximum annual rent of £50.

Perhaps the most interesting of the extensions of the borough's power contained within the charter was the right to establish what was referred to as a Pie Powder Court.

This right was tied up with the confirmation of the borough's right to hold markets and fairs, and clearly refers to the problems associated with having an unknown and large group of itinerants in the town during those periods.

In the charter the King states

*And further to our more abundant grace, and certain knowledge and mere motion, we do give and grant to the aforesaid mayor, bailiffs and burgesses of our borough of Wigan aforesaid, and their successors, that they and their successors for the future for ever, may have, hold and keep, and have the power to be able to have, hold and keep yearly, in the vill or borough of Wigan aforesaid, one fair, to begin in and upon the 16th day of July, if it be not the Lord's Day and, if it be so, then upon the next day following, and to be yearly kept, and to continue for all such day of the beginning thereof aforesaid, and through two days next following, together with a Court of Pie Powder at the time of the same fair . . .*

The borough had, for centuries, enjoyed the privilege of holding its own Courts Leet, but they really only had jurisdiction over serious crimes and other crimes committed by residents of the borough. The

Pie Powder Court – from the Norman or French words for 'dirty feet' – allowed the bailiffs and burgesses to try and fine travellers coming into the borough. Apparently considerable profit was gleaned from the proceedings which followed!

Wigan, therefore, approached the closing decades of the seventeenth century with all her ancient rights restored. The borough was once again in favour with the government, and busily engaged in rebuilding the damage done by so many years of war. During that war, the action which took place in and around the town may not have had the historic aura of Marston Moor, Naseby or Worcester, but in determing the outcome of twenty turbulent years, it had been no less important.

The charter in which the King recognised the importance of Wigan's loyalty to his cause survives in the Record Office in Leigh.

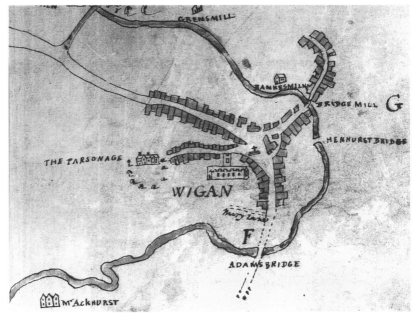

*A section of an 18th-century map which includes one of the earliest known representations of Wigan. This map was drawn up in 1712 to illustrate the proposed River Douglas Navigation, which accounts for the fact that the river and the watermills on its banks are shown prominently. [reproduced by permission of the Lancashire County Archivist, L.R.O. DP 175.]*

Chapter Five

# Eighteenth-century Wigan

The humble petition of James Bullock, Taylor, on behalf of himself
and the rest of the Taylors freemen of the said Borough . . . Sheweth,
– that Robert Bailey, John Moreton and Ralph Weedale, Taylors, have
lately, without any right or authority whatsoever, come into the said
Borough, and do exercise and practise their Trades in the said
Borough, to the great detriment of your Petitioner and others, and in
open defiance of the good and salutary Laws of this your Corporation.
Your Petitioner therefore, humbly prays that they may be redressed
and relieved according to the Circumstances of this Case, and as your
Worship thinks meet and proper.
*Verdict* – We order Robert Bayley, John Moreton and Ralph Widows
each to remove in a month's time, or forfeit thirty nine Shillings each,
and ye said sum for every month they stay afterwards.

The humble petition of Thomas Chadwick, Linen Weaver, Showeth, –
that your Petitioner is in very good circumstances, has no family, and
is desirous to inhabit and follow his Trade in your Corporation, and
for that purpose to be admitted as a freeman thereof, he being willing
to pay such a sum of money for his freedom as your Worships and the
Gentlemen of the Jury think proper. Your Petitioner therefore, humbly
prays you . . . that he may be admitted a freeman of this your
Corporation . . .
*Verdict* – We elect him a Freeman of this Corporation, he paying Four
Pounds four shillings in a month's time to the present Bailiffs.
Petitions laid before the Court Leet, January 1742.

 ROM the reign of Elizabeth I, Wigan was granted six
charters over a period of two and a half centuries, and
all still survive in the Record Office in Leigh. After
that of Charles II, the next charter, and one of the most
important in terms of the structure of local government within the borough, was that by James II, issued
in 1685. In that lengthy – and often repetitive – document, the
composition of Wigan's local governing body is defined and
enumerated. Thirty 'councillors' are listed – including mayor, recorder
(town clerk), ten other aldermen and eighteen 'capital burgesses' –
effectively borough councillors. The borough was required to keep
official records of its proceedings, and was empowered to make,
change and remove local by-laws. To facilitate this, the mayor and all
subsequent mayors were made justices of the peace.

In the event of a capital burgess dying in office or being removed from office, the mayor and burgesses were empowered to elect a replacement. The wording of this part of the charter is interesting as, for the first time, it makes it possible for one not necessarily from the large traditional group of voting burgesses – numbering between one and two hundred at the time of Charles I – to be elected to the council. The actual wording was:

> *It shall be lawful for the Mayor and Common Council of the said borough . . . to elect one or other of the inhabitants of the borough aforesaid in place of him or them being dead or so removed.*

For the election of aldermen, the charter affirmed that such office was only open to those already burgesses.

With this charter, therefore, Wigan had a borough council with an extended range of powers and authority. In many respects – but not in electoral terms – it was not unlike its modern-day equivalent. From the 1685 charter, no more would be granted to the town until 1832, in the reign of William IV. During the intervening century and a half, Wigan, while endeavouring to rebuild and expand its commercial importance, was once again in the midst of national turmoil.

The new King's 1685 charter opened up a whole new era in Wigan's civic development, and granted the borough powers to control and influence that development – some of them perhaps over-protective and restricting. The council could encourage commercial expansion and development, but it could also just as easily restrict it by limiting the freedom of trade and freedom of movement of the townspeople and merchants.

The new charter's powers, both civic and political, were welcomed in the town, but that was not the only aspect of James' accession which at least some influential Wiganers welcomed. James was a Catholic – he had quite openly admitted his conversion to Catholicism in 1672, although his daughters Anne and Mary were brought up Protestants. In fact, many of the leading families of the town were themselves Catholic, although some more openly than others. However, the new King, while full of religious zeal, was short of political tact.

Whatever hopes of better times the Catholic families of Wigan might have had, though, were dashed within three years. In 1673, the Test Act had made it illegal for either Catholics or nonconformists to hold high office, although in practice it was usually directed more vigourously towards Catholics than others. Thus, there was a strong sense of parliamentary disapproval over James becoming king, although less noticeable among the ordinary people. When the Dukes of Monmouth and Argyll independently sought to implement rebellion against him, for example, they found little support from the general public. In Parliament, the desire to replace the King was, however, considerable.

This became even stronger, when in 1687 James excluded Catholics from the terms of the 1673 Act and installed many in positions of power. Later he extended the exclusion to persuade the nonconformists to support him. Catholics returned to high state office, Mass was celebrated openly, and the largely Protestant Parliament – Whigs and Tories alike – were outraged. When James had a son in June 1688 – thus suggesting that there might even be a Catholic succession to the throne – an invitation was sent to William of Orange and Mary, James' sister. William landed in England in November 1688 and James fled, attempting to make his way to France. Despite being captured by William, James was allowed to escape, and made his way over the Channel. James returned to claim his throne in the following year and was defeated at the Battle of the Boyne, returning to France where he died in exile in 1701.

Several attempts to restore him to the throne were hatched and organised at Standish Hall, in a hollow between Wigan and Standish – the first around Christmas 1689 and New Year 1690. Not surprisingly, considerable secrecy surrounded the Christmas get-together. Those who were not invited knew nothing of the event, and those who were present were bound by an oath of secrecy. The men who gathered there had a common mission – a mission which, had it been successful, would have changed the story of British monarchy and politics for ever. In their midst, however, was a spy.

The deposed Stuart monarch had many loyal subjects throughout the country – some were drawn to his cause for religious reasons, some from simple loyalty, and others because they could not see the right in placing William and Mary on the throne as long as there was a Stuart male alive with a direct claim to the throne. The Catholic/Protestant divide was perhaps at its widest in this controversy, with the Catholic families of Lancashire in the forefront of organised objection to the installation of the Protestant William of Orange as king, albeit sharing

*Proclamation for the Apprehension of the Standish Plotters, 1690.*

*A line drawing of Standish Hall*

the throne with his Stuary Queen Mary.

Standish Hall was in many ways an ideal location was scheming against the new king. It was in Lancashire, where Stuart loyalties were still held by many; and it was a relatively easy location from which to reach many other parts of the country. William Standish was certainly not alone in the neighbourhood in wishing to see the Stuarts return to the throne, and many of the local families were represented at the Christmas and New Year house party. The Gerrards of Bryn, the Tyldesleys, the Stanleys, the Towneleys of Towneley Hall, the Daltons of Thurnham and others were represented, together with many lesser families, some military leaders and a scattering of priests.

Their plan was simple: to raise military and civilian support for King James II, who would ultimately return to England in triumph, to be met by increasingly large sympathetic forces as he moved south through Lancashire and back to London.

It was never to be, for, also present at Standish Hall was one Robert Dodsworth who, while apparently as fervent in his Jacobite sympathies as the others, was in fact an informer on the King's payroll. With details of the planned rebellion reaching Whitehall almost as soon as they had been discussed in Lancashire, the plot was doomed to fail. By May 1690, a royal proclamation had been issued for the arrest of the main players in the rebellion game. Dodsworth had been a good informer, for his king was able to list a total of thirty-six people who had hatched the plot.

'Whereas their Majesties have received information upon Oath that the persons herein after particularly named have conspired together with other disaffected persons to raise Rebellion', William and Mary proclaimed, 'their Majesties have thought fit to issue out this, their Proclamation', a proclamation which went on to name all those under suspicion and to issue severe threats as to what would happen to anyone who aided or abetted them!

It is an illustration of the inadequacy of communication and transport, of policing and indeed of order in England in the late-seventeenth century that apparently not one was arrested and, indeed, after an absence of only a year, William Standish was back at his ancestral home – preparing a second attempt to restore a Stuart king.

The plot hatched between 1692 and 1694 may have been better planned, but it was no more successful. It was, however, on a much more impressive and dramatic scale. Not only was an army to be raised to support the return of King James, but the current incumbent, William III, was to be assassinated to ease the restoration of the Stuart claimant. Yet again, however, information was leaked before plans were finalised – this time, apparently, by one John Lunt together with a John Womball, both of whom had been employed to help in the amassing of a huge armoury at Standish Hall ready for the planned uprising.

This time, in addition to the familes implicated in 1690, the Dicconsons, the Cliftons and others were involved. While the 1690 proclamation had listed all of those involved, the 1694 warrant mentioned only William Standish – for by the time government troops had arrived at Standish Hall, William, his followers and their cache of arms had been removed to a secret location.

*A Jacobite treasure – this James II locket contains what is reputed to be a lock of the Old Pretender's hair.*

King William III, from Kensington Palace, issued a warrant for his namesake's arrest, as follows:

*Whereas his Majesty hath received Information That William Standish of Standish Hall in the County of Lancaster hath Conspired, with divers other Disaffected Persons to Disturb and Destroy the Government, and for that purpose bought up Arms and Abetted and Adhered to his Majesties Enemies; for which cause several Warrants have been Issued for the Apprehending of the said William Standish, but he hath withdrawn himself from his usual Place of Abode and is fled from Justice.*

William managed to evade the King's officers and, despite a substantial reward being offered for information as to his whereabouts, was never arrested, although many of his friends and colleagues were apprehended in the summer of 1694 and imprisoned in Manchester.

That he was able to avoid capture for so long says much for the powerful attachment that most Lancastrians seem to have had for the Jacobite cause – most of whom would not actually raise rebellion themselves, but certainly would not betray to the authorities those who did.

The Jacobite Trials were among the most celebrated legal events of their time and achieved considerable notoriety. The outcome was the freeing of all the defendants and the withdrawal of the arrest warrant for William Standish, with distinct suggestions that much of the evidence against them had been circumstantial and perhaps drummed up for material gain rather than political reasons. There is also the possibility that King William, seeing the immediate threat recede, decided that the best way to de-fuse the situation would be to show clemency and forbearance to those who had been implicated in the various plots against him.

The plots had been real enough, however, and workmen on the Standish estates two and a half centuries after dug up a bundle of coded letters and papers which enabled historians to prove once and for all that the plot had been serious, well prepared and well funded. Cleared of suspicion of treason and conspiracy, William Standish returned to his home in 1695 and lived the rest of his life in what passed for peace in those days.

The King left several children as a result of two marriages – one to a Protestant, the other to a Catholic princess. While his two daughters, Mary and Anne, would in their time both become queens, his son by Mary of Modena, James Stuart (known as the Old Pretender and known by his friends as James III) would cause the north of the

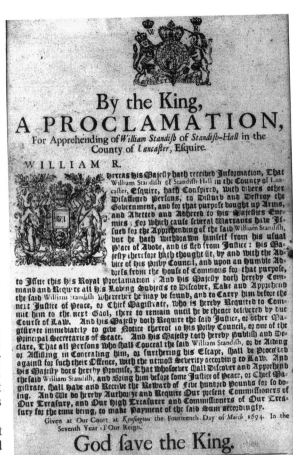

*While the 1690 royal proclamation was directed against a whole group of plotters, the 1694 version sought only the arrest of William Standish. This concentration of effort did not, however, produce the desired effect, for William was never apprehended.*

*Jacobite ivory and filigree writing tablets, now preserved in the local heritage collection.*

country to be thrown into a turmoil of war once again. The Jacobite movement, intent on putting James III on the throne, was gathering momentum.

William III was succeeded on the throne by Queen Anne, and when she died in 1714, George I, Elector of Hanover became King, and the Jacobites saw this as their best opportunity to make their bid for power.

In 1715 there were demonstrations in his favour in Manchester – where there was a considerable Jacobite presence and secret meetings took place in John Shaw's club. Wigan, however, was split. Several families were strongly pro-Jacobite, but they were in the minority.

By the end of October 1715, the Jacobite army, with promises of considerable support in Lancashire, was moving south from Scotland, intent on putting James III on the throne. At Lancaster, James III was proclaimed King, and the army continued its move south towards Preston. The Hanoverian armies under General Carpenter moved north to meet them, passing through Wigan in early November 1715, joined up with General Will's army which had crossed over from Yorkshire, and met the Jacobites in battle at Preston on November 13th. A few days later, the bedraggled remains of the defeated Jacobite army, many of them in chains, were marched back south through Wigan to London and imprisonment. Five Jacobite sympathisers from local families were publicly executed in Wigan.

When, thirty years later, the Jacobite cause was fought for once again – this time in an effort to put James' son Charles Edward Stuart on the throne, Wigan was once again in the army's path. This time it was to witness the retreat of the Jacobite forces north from Manchester.

Bonnie Prince Charlie's armies had moved south along the line of today's A6 in early November 1745, almost thirty years to the day since the last attempt. They recruited heavily throughout Lancashire, and especially from Wigan and Manchester. Marching as far south as Derby, the army had been swelled from about five thousand to about six thousand men, but at Derby they were warned that they were marching into a well-laid trap. By that time, also, they had been disappointed by the fact that the English rank and file had not rallied to their cause. Intelligence also told them that two vast armies had been assembled to confront him – one commanded by General Cumberland and the other by General Wade. Deciding to retreat rather than face annihilation from Cumberland's forces, the Jacobites turned north again, returning through Manchester and turning west to march through Wigan. All along the way, their numbers were gradually depleted as supporters returned to their homes and their families. Following the heavy defeat at Culloden, and the savage repression that came after it, the Jacobite cause was effectively dead.

The local families returned to their commercial endeavours – many of them involved in coal mining. As Catholics, they were excluded from civic and political office, so devoted their energies to farming, commerce and industry, and of course, to the Church. The Dicconsons, for instance, developed at least four collieries in the Wrightington and Shevington areas, and there is evidence of them having developed coking plants in the area as well. The foundations of an eighteenth-century coking oven were discovered when the M6 was being driven through Shevington in the 1960s. Edward Dicconson went on to become a bishop.

Eighteenth-century Wigan was at a crossroads in more ways than one. Quite literally it was at a major road junction, and that location had been the justification for its very existence for seventeen centuries. It was also at a crossroads in terms of its industrial development, for the route to real industrial progress was hampered by the lack of easy and effective transportation to and from the town. Although it was on the main road, this was a relatively narrow and often impassable route north or south. In an Act of Parliament of 1720, aimed at alleviating some of Wigan's transportation problems, the road was described as almost impassable. The Act noted that:

> *by reason of the many carriages of goods and merchandise passing through the same, [the roads] are become ruinous and almost impassable, especially in the winter season, and some parts thereof are so narrow that coaches and carriages cannot pass by one another.*

Acts of Parliament were necessary to empower the borough council and others to repair and re-lay the roads. Two such Acts were passed in 1720, one for the re-laying of the road north to Preston, the other for the road south to Warrington. In order to raise the funds, the decision was made to create turnpike roads – with tolls being charged for right of passage. In due course, toll houses were erected up Wigan Lane, at the foot of Wallgate, near the Millgate Bridge and at several other locations.

Writers of about this period, describing Wigan and mentioning the Wallgate Bar, the Standishgate Bar, the Millgate Bar and others, have often been presumed to have been talking about the medieval gates to a walled town. Much more likely is that they were referring to gates which marked the division between the end of turnpike roads and the beginning of the streets of Wigan – which were, of course, under council control. These bars, some of which dated back centuries, had two purposes. Previously they had been erected to collect dues or tolls which the rector in past centuries, and the council in seventeenth- and eighteenth-century Wigan were empowered to collect from merchants and travellers entering the town during its markets and fairs. When the road improvements were instigated, however, the toll gates would be in daily rather than occasional use. They would therefore require toll keepers and toll houses as well as just barriers.

Similarly, nineteenth-century writers commenting on the powers of the council in the late-seventeenth and the eighteenth centuries to restrict passage in and out of the town, have commented on the fact that councillors and aldermen required official permission to leave the town. What is probably the true reason behind such permits may have had less to do with the right of passage *per se*, than with the right of passage toll free if on council business!

*Right – Shevington Basket pit, seen here in the 1880s, continued a tradition which was a century old. Later pits replaced the baskets with the much safer cages. Records tell of horrendous injuries to miners descending in baskets – so constricted was the space that they could only have one leg in the basket when it was lowered – the other was free to collide with the rough hewn side of the shaft, or, indeed, get trapped against it.*

There were so many exclusions from the requirement to pay tolls in any case, that it might have been briefer to enumerate the situations under which tolls must be paid, rather than to list the exemptions! Exclusions included:

*gravel or other materials for repairing the said road or any roads in the parishes or townships in which the roads to be repaired do lie . . . or for carrying . . . any lime, dung, mould, or compost of any nature whatsoever for the manuring of any gardens or lands within the said parishes . . . nor for any wagons, carriages or carts carrying any hay, or corn in the straw, to be laid up in the houses, barns or outhouses of the respective inhabitants of the said parishes . . . nor for ploughs, harrows, or other implements of husbandry . . . any horses, geldings or mares, mules or asses going to or returning from any coal pit . . . going to or returning from any place of divine worship on Sundays, or with any corpse to be buried . . . for any post horse carrying the mail . . . or carriages going to or returning empty from the said towns of Wigan and Preston . . . nor for any wagon or cart . . . made use of in the drawing or carrying of corn, grain, meal or flour to or from any corn mill . . .*

As has already been noted, Wigan had turned its hand to a wide variety of manufacturing industries from the fourteenth century. Eighteenth-century Wigan was no different, except in the scale of these undertakings. Pewter ware, clocks, iron founding, smithing and a wide variety of other industries were carried on in the town, together with the two which were already establishing themselves as the mainstays of the town's economy – the coal and textile industries.

While medieval mining had been carried out on what were really no

more than small scale open cast sites – often in backyards – by the sixteenth century mining was mostly underground. Indeed, there is strong evidence that underground mining in the Orrell and Standish areas had been going on since the closing years of the sixteenth century at the very latest, and the output of some mines was of the order of one to two thousand tons annually before the end of the seventeenth century. Although underground workings were commonplace before the end of the seventeenth century they were in many cases drift mines – with sloping roads from the surface extending further downwards as the seams ran deeper. In some cases the working, while not very deep by later standards, were a long walk from the surface.

References to pit ponies in the list of exclusions from toll charges on the Wigan to Preston road clearly suggests that these animals were already in common use in the mines by 1720 – otherwise they would not have been mentioned.

Ventilation shafts were driven straight down into the workings, and these shafts – or wider ones – were used to haul the coal to the

*Brick making thrived in the town from the eighteenth to the twentieth centuries. Until the early years of this century, the bricks were usually hand-made*

surface in wicker baskets. As colliery technology developed, the deeper mines used the baskets, hauled by pit-head winding gear, to raise and lower both miners and coal. One colliery – often referred to as the 'Shevington Basket Pit' was still using this technique well into the nineteenth century and therefore gives us a rare photograph of what these mines looked like on the surface.

Certainly by the middle of the seventeenth century, the Standish estates were being deep mined extensively – by the Standishes themselves, and by the Heskeths and Dicconsons under licence. Nearer to Wigan, there had been a colliery at the foot of Millgate since the sixteenth century, and one often repeated local story tells of the problems the residents at the foot of Millgate and Chapel Lane experienced with coal-laden water, pumped from the pit after flooding during heavy rains, running down the street, in through their back doors and out again through the front!

Traditionally, much of the coal had been mined for domestic use rather than to be exported out of the area. A long tradition of iron founding required coking coal, and, as we have seen, early coke ovens which would have supplied that need have been discovered in recent years. With a growing demand for fuel nationally, the abundance of high quality coal – Wigan cannel had a reputation well beyond the boundaries of the borough long before it was exported from the town – determined that mining would be one of the industries which would secure Wigan's prosperity for as far into the future as any man could envisage. Just how important coal would become during the eighteenth century and into the nineteenth could not have been envisaged as the century opened. Equally, no one would have believed that a little over two centuries later, with much of the coal still underground, only vast unsightly open cast sites would remain.

The development of steam-powered pumping engines made significant improvements in conditions in mining nationally, and therefore made it practical to mine in locations which would otherwise have been impossible. A rising demand for coal ran parallel to the development of these engines. When James Watt patented the mechanism which converted the vertical motion of the steam engine into a rotary motion, the scene was set for an expansion of the market for coal which no one could have foreseen.

The textile industry too was expanding, although the major advances which made real mass production possible would come later in the century. Just as with coal, however, transportation proved to be the major bottleneck in the production cycle in the mid-eighteenth century. With raw wool and cotton coming into the town by road, and finished cloths being taken away again by the same means, quantities could never be particularly large. Transportation of the coal and the cotton remained the single large obstacle to their real exploitation. That clearly identified need is where the third Act of Parliament of 1720 originated.

In collaboration with landowners, mine owners and others, the councillors of Wigan determined to make the River Douglas navigable from the Ribble to Wigan. This was not a civic project, but a commercial undertaking by local businessmen, with the undoubted support of their civic leaders. It was certainly a commercial gamble, but it was also a far-sighted and important gesture of faith in the town's commercial future. It was not, however, the first such project. Eight years before this Act was presented to the Commons, legislation

*The Douglas Navigation predated the Leeds and Liverpool Canal by half a century and was the first successful attempt to link Wigan with the sea. River locks created, in effect, a series of long pounds down the river to the sea; no towpath was provided and we know that manpower was used to haul the boats upstream. This is the original plan for the navigation, drawn up by engineer, Thomas Steers, in 1712. The representation of Wigan in the top right corner is probably the earliest map of the town we have. The estuary of the River Ribble is on the far left.*
*[reproduced by permission of the County Archivist, Lancashire Record Office; L.R.O. DP 175.]*

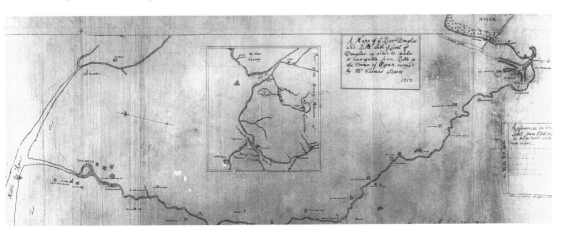

allowing a similar project had been thrown out by the Lords. At that time the River Douglas had been surveyed to test the feasibility of the proposed navigation, so the council in proposing their ambitious plans in 1720 already had a good idea that their project was practicable. It was also potentially very profitable, The Act laid down the terms upon which the navigation could be used . . .

> *And be it further enacted by the authority aforesaid that, for and in consideration of the great charge and expenses the said undertakers, their heirs or assigns, shall be at, not only in making the said River Douglas, alias Asland, navigable as aforesaid, but also in making, erecting, repairing, cleansing maintaining, keeping up, and continuing the weirs, locks, dams, sluices, bridges, cranes, wharfs, and other matters necessary to be made and erected aforesaid, it shall be and may be lawful to and for the said undertakers . . . to ask, demand, recover, and take, to and for their own proper use and behoof, in respect of their charges and expenses aforesaid, for all and every such coal, cannel, stone, slate, and other goods, wares, merchandises and commodities whatsoever, as shall be carried or conveyed in any boat, barge, or other vessel in, upon to, or from any part of the said River Douglas alias Asland between the said River Ribble to the town of Wigan, or down the said river, from the said town of Wigan, to the said River Ribble, any sum not exceeding two shillings and sixpence per ton, and so proportionately for every greater or lesser weight.*

No differences in the rate charged were permitted – but this was a charge for the right to use the waterway, not a carriage charge. That was a separate issue between boat owner and customer. The right of free passage for all the King's liege people – free in this sense meaning, unimpeded rather than without charge – was guaranteed . . .

> *in, along, through and upon the said River Douglas alias Asland or any part thereof between the said River Ribble and the place called Miry Lane End in the township of Wigan aforesaid, with boats, barges, lighters, and other vessels, and also the necessary and convenient liberties for navigating the same, without any let, hindrance, or obstruction from any person, whatsoever, paying such rate and duty, rates and duties, as are . . . to be paid . . .*

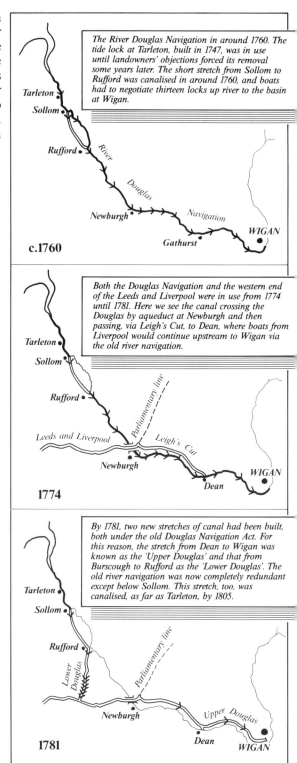

The River Douglas Navigation in around 1760. The tide lock at Tarleton, built in 1747, was in use until landowners' objections forced its removal some years later. The short stretch from Sollom to Rufford was canalised in around 1760, and boats had to negotiate thirteen locks up river to the basin at Wigan.

**c.1760**

Both the Douglas Navigation and the western end of the Leeds and Liverpool were in use from 1774 until 1781. Here we see the canal crossing the Douglas by aqueduct at Newburgh and then passing, via Leigh's Cut, to Dean, where boats from Liverpool would continue upstream to Wigan via the old river navigation.

**1774**

By 1781, two new stretches of canal had been built, both under the old Douglas Navigation Act. For this reason, the stretch from Dean to Wigan was known as the 'Upper Douglas' and that from Burscough to Rufford as the 'Lower Douglas'. The old river navigation was now completely redundant except below Sollom. This stretch, too, was canalised, as far as Tarleton, by 1805.

**1781**

Some rights were retained by the landowners along the way – particularly those of fishing and fowling. As the Douglas was a salmon river two and a half centuries ago, such rights and privileges were closely guarded.

With financial support from Sir Roger Bradshaigh, William Bankes and others, the great undertaking was commenced in 1732 and completed a decade later. The project was enormous. Locks had to be built at several points between Miry Lane and Tarleton, and a considerable quantity of local timber was used. In total, the project cost over twenty thousand pounds – a great deal of money at that time – and proved an immediate success. With the boats capable of carrying over forty tons, sometimes pulled by men, sometimes by horses, sometimes driven by wind, and at other times allowed to move downstream with the flow of the river, the passage of coal particularly was revolutionised.

The navigation also eased the transport of iron, bricks and a range of other commodities and, in doing so, fulfilled its creators' dreams of expanding Wigan as a major industrial centre. The same boats which carried Wigan produce downstream, returned laden with the raw materials for the town's expanding industries. The passage west had the tide to assist on occasions, but not always!

The job of pulling the boats back upstream to Wigan laden with raw cotton, flax and a variety of other materials, required teams of powerful horses – a task originally performed by teams of men since the cost of providing a towpath for horses was considered too expensive!

The cotton and flax helped the textile industry in the town develop out of all proportion to its seventeenth-century scale – and during the mid-eighteenth century there was a considerable development of weavers' housing in the town. Some of these houses stood until the 1960s in Wigan Lane.

The very success of the Douglas Navigation, however, proved its undoing, and after a working life much shorter than its backers might have expected, it was eclipsed by the dawn of the canal age. The Commissioners who were responsible for managing the river sold out to the Leeds and Liverpool Canal Company less than thirty years after the navigation had been completed. With a waterway now very much out of date, they must have considered themselves fortunate to be offered £14,000 – only six thousand pounds less than the building costs incurred thirty to forty years earlier.

Work started on the Leeds and Liverpool Canal in 1770 at both ends. Luckily, the Canal Company had purchased the right to take water from the headwaters of the Douglas when it had bought the old navigation, allowing the Lancashire end of the canal to be opened before the summit level and reservoirs were built. The route sanctioned by Parliament did not in fact pass through Wigan, since the Yorkshire promoters of the scheme were keen to build the shortest possible route to Liverpool. The Liverpool merchants, on the other hand, were determined to have easy access to the Wigan coalfield, and managed to have a clause inserted in the Act to allow a branch down to the Douglas Navigation at Dean (where traces of the old river lock can still be seen today), thereby giving access to Wigan. This much have been

highly successful, for by the time money was available for the completion of the Leeds and Liverpool across the Pennines and through East Lancashire, it was decided to alter the route to pass directly through Wigan. The whole canal was finally opened in 1816, some 46 years after construction began.

While the canal in its totality was a magnificent achievement – considering the technology and tools available at the time – the stretch between Wigan and Liverpool was the most significant as far as the development of the town was concerned. It gave Wigan industry easy access – and in bulk – to a major port for the first time. A spur to the River Douglas near Tarleton effectively replaced the Douglas Navigation and at the same time increased the maximum load on a single barge from forty to sixty tons.

The canal changed Wigan. In the decades which followed its construction, its route through the town dictated the siting and development of the major centres of manufacturing. Directly and indirectly it employed or was instrumental in the employment of thousands of people. The factories and mills which were built along its towpath in the nineteenth century would never have been there – might never have been built in Wigan – had the canal not been built.

In terms of commercial viability, the canal reduced the cost of bulk transportation by two-thirds compared with road haulage charges, and thus reduced the cost of Wigan produce significantly. In addition, the speed with which material could be moved by canal was a great deal faster than either road transport or the Douglas Navigation. Only nine locks separated Wigan from the docks at Liverpool, and it was relatively easy sailing, even in the days of horse-drawn boats. Bulk carriers could cover the thirty-five miles to Liverpool in twelve or thirteen hours, with Tarleton accessible in under eight. Moving eastwards from Wigan was a different matter, with the famous flight of twenty-three locks up to Kirkless starting just outside the town. Traffic eastwards never achieved the volume of that travelling west from the town. With the building of a branch to Leigh, access to the Duke of Bridgewater's canal and the Midland canal network was achieved. In the nineteenth century easy access to the Manchester Ship canal was added.

Most important was the integration of the canal into the existing local transport network. Most of the local collieries had horse-drawn tramways to move their coal from the pit heads, and these were extended to the canalside, giving rise to the proliferation of 'tipplers' or 'piers' which would later make Wigan famous in a very different way!

The export of Wigan coal in particular was the deciding factor in the success both of the town and of the canal. That bulk movement was eased, speeded up and increased – with direct access to Liverpool, and via Tarleton to Barrow and elsewhere – historically just at the right time. With Liverpool becoming the centre for the importing of cotton, raw materials could be delivered to Wigan mills less than a day after arriving in the port. At the time the canal was built, the true significance of that easy passage of goods – and especially coal – in bulk could not have been appreciated. The next century would demonstrate just how timely the construction of the canal had been.

*Wigan in 1827 – on the threshold of major expansion. To cater for the rapidly growing population and the expanding industrial base the once simple street plan is beginning to take on the shape of the modern town. In the following thirty years, with the arrival of the railway (see the map on page 120), the town expanded to several times this size. Skirting the east of the town, and at this date still running through relatively open countryside, can be seen the Leeds and Liverpool Canal. Of interest here is the 'canal feeder', the original water supply for the Liverpool end of the canal which was diverted from the Douglas near Scholes Bridge (the Canal Company had to purchase the right to use the headwaters of the Douglas from the old River Douglas Navigation Company). The original navigation's basin was still in use by the canal. The Leigh Branch, recently built, can also be seen.*

# The Canal

HE Leeds and Liverpool Canal, opened as far as Wigan in 1779, had a tremendous influence on the development and history of the town in the nineteenth and twentieth centuries. Its opening created an essential transport system for coal and cotton, providing easy access to mines and mills alike. To an extent it replaced the Douglas Navigation which had been in existence for fifty years or so before the canal was constructed. When it is considered that the 'cut' was largely dug out with picks and shovels, the engineering is awesome. As a means of getting raw materials to Wigan, and Wigan's produce to Liverpool, it was highly successful, although the decision to use a narrower cut and shorter boats from Wigan to Leeds did restrict its use as a cross-Pennine waterway. It continued in reasonably heavy until after the Second World War, but is today largely used by pleasure craft. The regeneration of the Wigan Pier basin has turned it into one of the country's most successful heritage centres and tourist attractions.

*Above, left: Crooke Tippler – as well as the now famous 'Wigan Pier', there were several coal staithes or 'tipplers' on the canal, loading barges directly from the town's many mines.*

*Above: Wigan Canal Basin – today the canal basin is the site of the Wigan Pier complex – and a thriving tourist attraction.*

*Left: This photograph of around 1902 reminds us that leisure use of the canal is nothing new.*

*Right, top: Wigan Canal Basin – in its more run-down period, the deserted wharfs and warehouses were such a blot on the town's image that serious consideration was given to demolishing them in the 1970s.*

*Right, bottom: Flyboats – these 'fast' barges carried a wide variety of produce across the Pennines.*

Chapter Six

# Coal and steam

**In the neighbourhood of this town is found that kind of coal they call Canell or Candle Coal, which, though they are found here in great plenty, and are very cheap, are yet very singular; for there are none such to be seen in Britain, or perhaps in the world besides. They so soon take fire, that, by putting a lighted candle to them, they are presently in a flame, and yet hold fire so long as any coals whatever, and more or less, as they are placed in the grate or hearth, whether flat or edged, whether right up and down, and polar, or level and horizontal.**
**They are smooth and slick when the pieces part from one another, and will polish like alabaster; then a lady may take them up in a cambric handerchief and they will not soil it, though they are as black as the deepest jet. They are the most pleasant, agreeable fuel that can be found, but they are remote; and though some of them have been brought to London, yet they are so dear, by reason of the carriage, that few care to buy them . . .**

Daniel Defoe
*A Tour Through the Whole Island of Great Britain* (1725)

*Carved cannel portrait of Colonel Blundell of Pemberton Colliery. The cannel coal of the Wigan area had remarkable properties, quite apart from burning well, producing little ash and great heat..*

EVELOPMENTS in mining were advancing at such a pace towards the end of the eighteenth century that demand for mining machinery was almost out-stripping production capacity. The mid-eighteenth century had seen a rapid move from drift mining to mines with vertical shafts, albeit not very deep. The abundance of coal relatively near the surface made possible the opening of mines with shafts less than a hundred feet deep – though still a fair depth considering they had to be dug by hand. It was common practice to sink a number of shafts so that the distance from the workings to the foot of a shaft was never very great. This was necessary for a number of reasons. First and most important was ventilation; there was no easy method of mechanical ventilation of the mines, so a profusion of air shafts would have been necessary anyway. Combining two roles in a single shaft – ventilation and the transportation of coal to the surface – made economic sense. Secondly, in the eighteenth century, the systems for the transportation of coal underground were rather primitive. There were, as yet, few under-ground tramways or railways, and coal was traditionally moved in small trucks pushed or pulled along the underground roadways by men and sometimes by children.

*Cannel portrait of Lord Lindsay – despite the esteem in which cannel was normally held, George Orwell described it as 'another inflammable rock called cannel . . . it makes tolerable fuel, not good enough to be commercially valuable.'*

With a huge expansion of mining – something approaching a thousand shafts of one sort or another were sunk in and around the Wigan coalfield before the end of the eighteenth century – there was an unprecedented increase in the demand for the equipment needed to operate those mines – trucks, rails, winding gear, pumps and a host of other items.

In Wigan, to go somewhere towards meeting that demand, Haigh Ironworks opened in 1790 and, despite high haulage costs from the foundry to the mines and particularly to the canal, machinery from the factory was sold widely throughout the country.

This was but the latest development in a long tradition of metal working within the town. Pewter ware had been made in Wigan for centuries, and the town already had a high reputation for bell founding. It is interesting to note that with the advance of mining and textiles, the old industries of bell making and pewter ware, together with pottery, once a mainstay of the town's economy, died out within a relatively short period of time.

Haigh Ironworks had the local rights to build steam pumping engines – Cornish engines, Newcomen engines and later the more powerful Boulton and Watt engines – and these became increasingly in demand as the number of new mines being sunk increased. Wigan mines were always wet and always suffered from gas problems. The sandstone through which the shafts had to be sunk retained water and, of course, as soon as this was penetrated, water drainage down into the workings became a major problem. Steam pumping engines were being installed in local mines before the end of the eighteenth century, and installed in considerable numbers.

The first commercial steam engines for driving factory machinery had been introduced by about 1790 and, in this respect, Wigan was very slow to adapt to the new machinery and methods. While Manchester and even Bolton had steam-powered textile machinery before the end of the eighteenth century, Wigan's textile machines, such as they were, were still operated manually. Thus, Wigan was exporting coal to power steam driven mules and power looms in towns with whom it was in direct competition, while its own spinning and weaving industry was still based on hand-operated spinning and handloom weaving.

The advent of steam power and the opening of the canal date from approximately the same time. So the real expansion of the coal business started at about the same time as the completion of the first stage of the Leeds and Liverpool Canal in the 1770s, between 1774 and 1779. In the late 1770s, Liverpool merchants were making deals with Wigan colliery owners for the bulk purchase of coal, especially cannel. One such deal – between the Liverpool company of Samuel Warren & Company and several local mineowners – was for 7,000 tons of cannel per year for seven years, at the rate of 5d. (2p) per basket, each basket holding about twenty stone.

Considering that a few years earlier there were few pits with an annual output of over two thousand tons, a single deal on this scale – and before the steam age really started – demonstrates just how great the demand for fuel had rapidly become. One of the partners in Warrens – Jonathan Blundell – headed a family which would itself become one of Wigan's major colliery owners, developing the giant Pemberton Colliery which continued in production until the middle of this century.

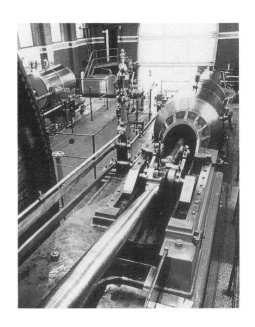

*Above – Fully restored steam engines at Trencherfield Mill.*
*Below – An eleven ton block of cannel brought out of Junction Colliery in 1880.*

The canal, having been constructed from Liverpool eastwards towards Wigan, reached the Orrell and Shevington coalfields by 1774, giving the owners in that area a head start of nearly five years in exploiting the canal as a transportation system. For collieries nearer the town, the Douglas Navigation or road haulage remained their transport options. Indeed, at the time the Liverpool to Gathurst section had been opened, arguments were still raging over whether or not Wigan should be linked to the canal at all!

At the end of the eighteenth century, mines were on an altogether smaller scale than today. There are records, in the 1790s, of pits with an annual output of two thousand tons being worked by only four or five miners, with an equal number of men at ground level working the pumps, moving the coal trucks and so on. Many of the larger collieries employed only about a dozen men underground, with perhaps as many again on the surface, producing six or seven thousand tons of coal annually. The days of mines employing men in their thousands were still some time in the future.

While huge investment was being made in an expansion of mining in and around the town, little investment was being made in

*Wigan's Pit Brow girls posed readily for the cameras of local photographers. This hand-coloured postcard was on sale in the years before the Great War.*

**Above** – *More pit girls pose in front of the winding gear of Junction Colliery.*
**Below** – *Wigan Market – a hand-coloured photograph of Wigan's famous Friday market, taken about 1904.*

**Above** – The Old Dog *in Market Place. The caption is by Whitehouse and says 'where Derby hid'.*
**Below** – *Thomas Whitehouse's residence in Millgate, now a furniture warehouse.*

**Above** – The Royal Hotel *and the* Eagle & Child, *Whitehouse.*
**Below** – *Wigan Market Place, also by Whitehouse.*

**Above** – *The residence of the Grammar School headmaster, built in 1693.*
**Below** – *Wigan Parish Church, painted by Whitehouse in 1826.*

**Above** – *Market Place, also by Whitehouse.*
**Below** – *Wigan Lane. From Thomas Whitehouse's illustrations for his manuscript history of Wigan in the 1830s.*

**Above** – *Two photographs of Wigan Pier in 1970 showing the Pier warehouses as they were then, abandoned by the community and due, it was thought, for demolition.*
**Below** – *Sixteen years later, Wigan Pier emerged from a multi-million pound restoration project as one of the leading tourist attractions in the county. The picture below, taken in 1989, shows Wigan Pier Heritage Centre and the replica coal 'tippler' which became known as Wigan Pier.*

**Top** – *The top of Market Street as seen about 1905. Many such postcards were produced of the town – by Will Smith of Wigan Lane, and by Starrs of Wigan.*
**Left** – *Wigan looks to the future – the tower of the new Galleries shopping precinct will dominate the town's skyline into the next century.*
**Above** – *Lindsay, the last surviving locomotive built by Wigan Coal & Iron Company, built over a hundred years ago and, thanks to painstaking restoration, likely to run for many years.*

upgrading manufacturing processes. With such a lead in the mining industry, one might have expected a pioneering spirit in the use of steam to have been adopted by the owners of Wigan's factories.

The use of steam traction was first introduced in 1804 when Richard Trevithick's mounted what had been a stationary steam engine on to a four-wheeled chassis and ran it on the tramway used to haul iron from the Penydarren Ironworks at Abercynon to the nearby Glamorgan Canal. This nine-mile-long track became the first industrial railway to be hauled by a steam engine, and the demonstration train – hauling fifteen tons of iron – made several journeys in February of that year.

By the early years of the nineteenth century, Robert Dalglish had been appointed to run the Haigh Ironworks. Dalglish took on the management of a business which had developed supplying local collieries with a wide variety of rails, machinery and other equipment. His own enthusiasm for the work of James Watt, Richard Trevithick and others, however, led him in 1812 to develop at Haigh what became known as the Dalglish Walking Horse – the first steam engine to appear in Lancashire, only eight years after the Glamorgan demonstration, and seven years before steam first worked the Stockton and Darlington Railway. Based on a Blenkinsop design, Dalglish's six-wheeled engine must have caused quite a stir when it first appeared.

The Walking Horse was developed to mechanise the tramway which linked John Pit in Orrell with the Leeds and Liverpool Canal, running on a four foot gauge track built on stone blocks. A later locomotive, also built by Dalglish, hauled trucks from Lamb & Moore's Meadow Pit to Newtown.

*This page – The Blenkinsop locomotive – Dalglish improved this design for the first steam locomotive to run in Wigan.*

The Walking Horse was capable of hauling twenty trucks, each carrying one ton of coal, resulting in a significant speeding up of the process of moving the coal from the mines to the canal. A single locomotive could do the work of several horses.

There was a delight in steam traction – especially from the mine owners who had no fuel costs! Coal being used to power the means of hauling coal had a huge effect on the fortunes and outputs of local mines.

The idea of railways as a means of speeding up the carriage of both people and merchandise was not originated in the steam age, although the advent of steam power made it significantly more practical. Plans for developing a horse-drawn railway between Liverpool and Manchester had been mooted before the end of the eighteenth century, but never put into effect. With steam becoming more reliable in the early years of the nineteenth century, the plan was resurrected, but it was felt that locomotive development had not yet reached a point where the system could be guaranteed to operate regularly.

Stevenson's demonstrations on the Stockton and Darlington Railway changed all that – the railway generated a ten-fold increase in trade between the two towns – and the Liverpool to Manchester link became a reality. Work started in 1826 and the famous Rainhill Trials to test the relative merits of different locomotive designs took place in 1829, with the famous *Rocket* emerging victorious. By 1830 the line was open and travel time between Manchester and Liverpool had been reduced at a stroke by ninety per cent!

The canal companies were understandably horrified by these developments. Surprisingly, however, the railways were not able to compete for bulk cargoes like coal and traffic on the canal continued to increase. Nevertheless, for Wigan, the effect of the railways was profound. Both Wigan and Manchester shared the port of Liverpool as their main contact with the rest of the world. Now goods from Manchester could reach Liverpool in a fraction of the time by rail that Wigan's produce took to reach the same destination by canal.

Despite consistent growth, Wigan was rapidly being overtaken in terms of industrial importance – a process which had been going on for fifty years – and the advent of a railway link between its two major industrial neighbours and competitors could only further their industrial and commercial development at Wigan's expense. In the

*The Ince, built for the Ince Coal & Cannel Company for use at Douglas Bank Colliery. This splendid 0-4-OST was typical of a type used in many local collieries – the ready supply of coal meant that a large coal bunker on the locomotive was an unnecessary additional weight. When the crew needed coal, they just stopped by the nearest pile of the stuff and stoked the fire!*

early-seventeenth century, Liverpool, Manchester and Wigan had for a time been approximately the same size. Indeed, in earlier years Wiganers had often disparagingly referred to Liverpool as a village!

In 1700, Manchester had a population of only 7,000 people and Liverpool about 6,000. At the same time, Wigan – the parish, including the borough – boasted a population of about 6,000, so the three were about the same size. A century later it was a very different story. Both Liverpool and Manchester had populations around ten times that of Wigan borough, and nearly twice that of Wigan parish. While Wigan's population had doubled during the eighteenth century, the pace of industrial development, and the creation of jobs in both Liverpool and Manchester, had required those towns to expand rapidly – increasing their populations seven-fold in the process.

In the first three decades of the nineteenth century that trend continued, and the gap widened. Wigan borough's population increased from 11,000 in 1800 to 20,000 by 1830, while that of the parish increased from 25,000 to 45,000. In the same period, Liverpool grew from 77,000 to 165,000. Manchester was expanding at a similar rate – 70,000 in 1800 to 150,000 by the time the railway opened.

However, it would be quite wrong to interpret these statistics as evidence of a downturn in Wigan's fortunes. Quite the reverse was the case. A measure much beloved of the Victorians in determining the modernity of a town's industrial base was the number of working steam engines operating in a given year. In that respect, Wigan comes out well. Despite a slow start in converting to steam power for driving machinery, the town actually had more steam engines per head of population than either Liverpool or Manchester in 1830. By 1825, Liverpool had nearly eighty steam engines working in its factories, with over a hundred, five years later. Manchester at the same dates had slightly more, generating the equivalent of over three hundred horsepower. Wigan, with thirty-two in 1825 and fifty-five by 1830 – one hundred and ten if the entire parish is included – was actually mechanising faster than either of its larger neighbours. That gave Liverpool and Manchester each about one steam engine for every fifteen hundred people, while Wigan could boast one for every six hundred or so within the boundaries of the parish! The town was certainly making up for lost time earlier in the century!

Neither was it slow to develop a railway! Within two years of the opening of the L & M, the Wigan and Newton Railway was in operation, built at a cost of £70,000 and running from a station at Chapel Lane down to meet the L & M at Parkside near Newton-le-Willows. September 3rd 1832 saw the first train leave from the small station about two hundred yards from the present day North Western Station.

By 1840 there were thirty-nine known textile manufacturers in the town – two producing flax, the rest cotton, and at least seven thousand people were employed in the industry.

The mines accounted for approaching ten thousand more. The borough had its own waterworks – established in 1761, and a municipal gas works had been opened in 1823. There was, in fact, a considerable quantity of underground natural gas within the Wigan area as well, and the town had several celebrated 'burning wells',

*A studio portrait of a pit lass by Wragg of Wigan – images like this were available for sale. The idea of women working in coal mines obviously held considerable fascination in Victorian and Edwardian times*

particularly in the Hindley and Ince areas. First recorded in the sixteenth century, some of these burning wells can still be seen today as gases seep up to the surface.

Over fifty collieries were in operation in the neighbourhood, including those at Haigh, Ince, Aspull, Orrell, Winstanley and Pemberton. To the established trades had been added brick-making and nail-making. Iron was being mined at Haigh, and quarries were working around the borough.

Between 1835 and 1838, railway links were established north to Preston, and a new station built to replace the old terminus in Chapel Lane. The Lancashire & Yorkshire Railway reached the town in 1848 and gave Wigan its first direct rail link to Liverpool and Manchester. It

PIT BROW GIRLS 6.

*A turn of the century postcard showing pit lasses at work in the Arley Mines of the Moss Hall Colliery Company. Extensive series of postcards showing them at work – often hand-coloured – were sold widely throughout the country.*

was to be thirty years later before the third railway reached the town with the construction of the line to Central Station.

By the middle of the century, steam power was an established part of industrial life. Vast steam engines were needed to power the increasingly large mills which were being built in the town, and to keep them fuelled, large quantities of coal were being used.

The canal, eclipsed by the railway as a means of carrying general goods, was still leading the way in the carriage of coal. Much heavier loads could be moved more easily by boat than by railway, and by the 1850s, over half a million tons annually was being transported by barge. As a result of the easy carriage of coal and the ready supply of water, the giant mills were often sited by the canalside. It would be towards the end of the century before the haulage capacity of the railways, and of steam locomotives, prompted the first mill owner to build near the railway rather than the waterway.

Nineteenth-century mining was a far cry from the systems used in the sixteenth to eighteenth centuries, but in the first half of the century, it was still based solely on manual labour. The last thirty years of the century would see mechanisation come to mining as it had done to just about every other industry during the latter half of Victoria's reign.

Eighteenth-century mining had moved from a system of sloping drifts cut into the side of a hill to the seams relatively near to the surface, to the sinking of shafts a hundred or so feet vertically into the ground. Initially these had been worked in all directions, creating a sort of beehive shape at the foot of the shaft, the seam being worked until the entire structure was in imminent danger of collapse. A sophistication of this technique had evolved before the end of the eighteenth century where columns or pillars of coal were left in place to support the roof of the workings, allowing the extraction of much greater quantities of coal before collapse was likely. The next stage was the development of underground workings which proceeded along a seam, again leaving pillars of coal for support, but sinking new shafts every few hundred feet to simplify and speed up the transport of coal to

# Coal

**W**IGAN was – quite literally – built on coal. Coal was the basic industry of the town for centuries. Today, save for a few opencast sites, coal mining is a thing of the past. Looking at mineral maps of Wigan, the town and the surrounding area are peppered with over a thousand old shafts – mine shafts, air shafts and so on. The industry once employed over half the male workforce, and, on the pit brow, a considerable number of women. Many lives were lost in the mines over the years and many other lives shortened or damaged by the working conditions. The sites of many of the largest mines have been cleared, landscaped and turned over to residential use. Pits live on in the names of streets and pubs, but little else. Cannel coal, a coal that burned bright and hot with little ash, was the jewel in the crown of the Wigan coalfield. It was as smooth as jet to look at, and miners carved it into ornaments, trophies – and even a dinner service for Haigh Hall that was used to stoke the fire after the meal was over.

*Left: Miner coming home 1932 – Once a familiar sight in the town, the miner trudging through town after a shift is now a long, forgotten part of Wigan's past.*
*Below: Miners and ponies at Blundell's Colliery c1900.*
*Above, right: Miner at the Coalface – this postcard dated about 1905 was one of an extensive series on local mines and mining. Wigan mines were hot, damp and gaseous. The miners worked in incredibly cramped spaces – four feet of headroom was considered a luxury.*
*Right, bottom: Victoria Pit Boers Head – sinking a shaft in the 1890s.*

# The Railway Era

IGAN's railway network developed simultaneously on two fronts – a growing network of mineral lines to carry coal from the town's many mines, and later from cotton mills as well, and a passenger system based on three stations. North Western, originally opened to passengers in 1888 to replace an earlier station at Chapel Lane, was completely rebuilt in the 1970s when the west coast line was electrified and at the same time the number of platforms were reduced. Wallgate, Wigan's Lancashire & Yorkshire Railway Company station was opened in 1876 – the third L&YR station to be built in the town – neither of the other two had proved satisfactory. It too underwent rebuilding in the 1970s when the original canopy was replaced with the present very much shorter one. Central Station was the last of the three to be opened – by the Grand Central Railway in 1892 – and was closed in the sixties when the Scholes area was extensively redeveloped. Well into the '70s its site remained undeveloped but is now occupied by the Station Road multi-storey car park.

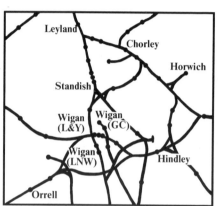

*Left: A glance at any railway map, or indeed an Ordnance Survey map of almost any period, immediately shows the complex network of railways that used to exist in the Wigan area.*
*Below: Wigan Central – a rare phorograph taken in the very early years of this century. This station replaced an earlier terminus in Darlington Street and the tracks connected with the Cheshire Lines Committee tracks, offering a somewhat circuitous alternative to the Wallgate–Manchester Victoria service.*
*Opposite, bottom: Railway Staff, North Western c1900 – The full station staff posed for a series of pictures. Behind them is a train of typical London & North Western Railway wooden bodied eight-wheel coaches.*

**Right:** *Railway Staff, North Western, c1989 – today's station staff pose for the author's camera.*

**Below:** *Accident at North Western* – The Illustrated London News *ran a lengthy story on this disaster. A night train travelling at about forty miles per hour came off the tracks at the original North Western station – a few yards from the present one – in August 1873, causing considerable injury and loss of life. Passengers were tended to according to their 'class', with third-class being given first aid on the platform, second-class in the waiting room and the VIPs being taken to the Royal Hotel! Twelve passengers were killed and several carriages finished up plunging through the roofs of nearby workshops.*

*The Alexandra pits sunk at Whelley were once considered to be deep mines by the standard of the day. Today, however, seams at that depth are often mined by open cast. This photograph shows the Alexandra opencast site in 1989. It is currently being restored now that the coal has been extracted.*

the surface.

In this century, many of the older workings, abandoned because they became too difficult or dangerous to work, are being exploited by huge opencast sites, and it is not uncommon for the opencast workings to reveal the abandoned remains of eighteenth- and nineteenth-century mines as the huge diggers tear away at the coal seams near to the surface.

As the easier seams became exhausted, the necessity for deeper shafts required a re-think of the working method. Thus, pit-head winding gear started to appear, ventilation for the deeper seams had to be organised, and drainage tunnels cut to keep the workings workable. By the end of the eighteenth century, two hundred foot deep shafts were not uncommon.

During the century, mines went very much deeper, the number of people employed in the industry sharply increased, and demand for coal from Victorian industry seemed insatiable. By the end of the century, a mineral map of Wigan showed over a thousand shafts of one sort or another, but what it could not show was the complex underground labyrinth of tunnels, roadways, drains and other workings, out of which several millions of tons of coal had been hewn by hand.

The first pits sunk by Blundell's at Pemberton in the early years of the nineteenth century were four hundred feet deep. By the 1860s, miners at the same site were working one thousand nine hundred feet below ground!

By the 1830s, mines were being sunk 500ft. to 800ft. deep – a phenomenal feat considering the shafts were entirely dug with picks and shovels. Indeed hand sinking of shafts was still common in the 1890s, despite the increasing availability of mechanical systems.

Mining has always been a dangerous job. The cost of coal has always involved a considerable loss of life. While the great mining disasters of the second half of the nineteenth century and of this century are most easily remembered because of the scale of the loss of life, earlier deaths perhaps were disproportionately large in their numbers, considering the size of the workforce involved. In their highly detailed accounts of the Standish coalfields published in 1984, Anderson, France and Lane list over one hundred deaths in the Standish pits alone between 1829 and 1837. A considerable number involved deaths caused by men and women falling down the unprotected shafts, but an even greater number – over sixty per cent of the total – involved the deaths of both men and women due to gas explosions below ground. In one instance in 1835 three sisters working deep in the Standish mines were all killed by a gas explosion – or an explosion of 'inflammable air' as the records preferred to describe it! Gas in Wigan mines was a perennial problem and in the years between the 1830s and the First World War claimed hundreds of lives. Despite that history, the mine owners at the time of the Maypole disaster in 1908 would deny that Wigan mines suffered either from damp or gas!

In mid century there was a clear distinction between coal and cannel, many companies listing themselves as 'Coal and Cannel' companies. Thus, in the 1841 Statistical Account for Lancashire is noted that the Wigan area had

> upwards of fifty collieries, chiefly in Haigh, Orrell, Winstanley and Pemberton; there are also several cannel mines, principally in Aspull and Ince.

*The last coal screen, at Lamb and Moore's Colliery, 1910. The overhead railway that led from this colliery in Scot Lane, Newtown, to the canal was the structure which became famous as Wigan Pier.*

The huge Standish coalfield was listed separately and included fifteen collieries, making a total of over seventy for the area. By 1870, that total had risen to over eighty and was producing something approaching five million tons a year – a far cry from the fifty to one hundred thousand tons a century earlier!

Among the pits being developed in the 1850s were Bankes' Winstanley pits and Lindsay's Alexandra pits in Whelley, both sunk in 1856. These were considered deep pits, at 800 feet, passing through seams of coal which were worked out and abandoned in the 1850s. The Whelley seams have recently been mined at the vast opencast site which dominated the area for the past few years. The shafts, only a few feet wide in the first deep mines, became wider and wider as the cages and hoists grew in size and the quantity of coal lifted out of the mine on each lift became greater. Eighteen and twenty foot wide shafts would soon become common. Also in the 1850s, Rose Bridge Colliery sank shafts to depths of a thousand feet for the first time.

By the late 1860s, and the sinking of the new shaft at the Caroline pit at Rose Bridge to a depth of two and a half thousand feet – the deepest in Britain at the time – made the existing pits on the site seem quite shallow by comparison!

All these deep mines were only practical thanks to the advent of steam power. Steam to work the winding gear, steam to work the ventilation fans, and steam to move the trainloads of coal, all made mining of a vast scale immediately possible. With the temperature at the coal face two thousand feet below ground a fairly constant and very humid 100°F (about 34°C), working at those depths would otherwise have been impossible.

Haigh Foundry was responsible for meeting a considerable part of the huge demand for steam engines, fans and winding gear, as was the Kirkless Iron Works and its successor, the Wigan Coal and Iron Company formed in 1865. Wigan Coal and Iron Company also went into the design and manufacture of steam locomotives in a major way. While it was the Haigh Ironworks which had pioneered locomotive building in the town. W.C. & I. had, by the 1860s, become the local market leader. Many local mineral lines echoed to the sound of their sturdy saddle tanks hauling long coal trains to the main lines, to the canal, or to other distribution points. One locomotive, *Lindsay,* an 0-6-0 saddle tank engine built in 1887, celebrated its centenary pulling trainloads of visitors at Carnforth steam centre in 1987. It has recently completed boiler repairs and is looking forward to working well into its second century.

As the Wigan Coal and Iron Company had developed locomotives, Haigh Foundry had developed an expertise for the design and construction of stationary engines and winding gear, and their expertise in casting large wheels and engine components later led to their involvement with the Vulcan Company in Liverpool as a sub-contractor in the casting and construction of the Laxey Wheel in the Isle of Man. In addition, factories opened up to supply the wagons needed in their hundreds – if not thousands – to ship the increasingly large output of the local mines.

The massive steam engines which were being installed in Wigan pits by the mid-nineteenth century were revolutionising the industry. By the 1870s with companies like the Haigh Foundry building huge twin 36-inch cylinder steam engines of immense power, winding engines were capable of hauling cages to the surface with the speed of an express train – speeds of over 50 mph are recorded. They also pumped vast quantities of air down into the pits. Without adequate ventilation, the mines could never have been worked, but that constant supply of oxygen-rich fresh air was in itself a hazard – if there was an explosion, the fresh air fuelled it. In the Maypole in 1908, the winds and fresh air well below ground – provided by the giant fans on the surface – actually assisted the rapid movement of the fireball after the explosion in its race through the underground roadways!

While the number of workers at the coalface moved into the thousands as the nineteenth century progressed, they were really only a relatively small proportion of the total number of people who relied on the mines for their livelihood. For every collier who worked underground, there were at least two workers on the surface. They moved the coal, worked the fans and the pumps, graded and loaded the coal, drove the trains which removed the coal from the pithead and so on. Wigan's network of mineral railways alone employed hundreds of men. Steam locomotives required drivers, firemen, fitters and a host of other ancillary workers. The drivers had to be trained to the same standard as those who drove the main line expresses which sped through Wigan on their way from London to Glasgow – for many of the mineral lines shared track with, or crossed over, the main railways.

Between them they extracted and transported an enormous amount of coal. In the 1870s, the Lancashire coalfield produced about seven million tons of coal – and as has been noted over five million tons of it came from the coalfields around Wigan.

The workforce exceeded ten thousand for the first time in the 1870s, of which a small, but important proportion were women. Nine-tenths of all working women in Wigan were employed in the mills and the remainder were just about evenly split between shops and mines. In Wigan in 1870, about five or six hundred women worked in the town's many collieries. That probably represented a much smaller proportion of the total workforce than had been made up by women fifty years earlier. Certainly at the turn of the century women and children were widely employed in mines, although the numbers involved were necessarily very much smaller.

The 'Pit Brow Lasses', from the early 1860s until the turn of the century, became the subject of many photographs which, because this form of female labour was unusual, to say the least, sold widely throughout the country. The pit lasses also attracted the attention of Arthur Munby, a Victorian eccentric who became somewhat obsessed by them. He once described Wigan as the picturesque headquarters of rough female labour and made a serious study of the pit girls and their hard lifestyle.

In 1859, on a visit to one of the Kirkless Hall pits near Hindley he wrote:

> *The black nondescript creatures pushing the waggons along the embankments would not be noticed by travellers on the [main railway] line; they would pass for men, but I recognised them at once as my stout hearty friends, the Lancashire collier girls. The costume of these girls and women is always the*

*same, and a good useful one it is. A hooded bonnet of padded cotton, pink blue or black; a blue striped shirt, open at the breast; a waistcoat of cloth, generally double breasted, but ragged and patched throughout; fustian or corduroy or sometimes black cloth trousers, patched with all possible materials except the original one; and stout clog shoon, brass clasped, on their bare feet; round the waist is tucked a petticoat of striped cotton, blue and black, rolled up as a joiners rolls his apron; it is never let down, and is perfectly useless – only retained as a symbol of sex. At the first pit I found four women, all young; one was standing with her hands in her pockets, and another sitting dangling her legs on the edge of a railway truck, waiting for coals from the pit's mouth to fill it. The third girl I found behind a great bank of coke, digging it down with a spade ready for the corves. While talking to her, a train of empty corves started down the slope towards us from the pits mouth; the fourth girl who was in charge of it, took a flying leap, as she set the train a going, and stuck on to one of the corves till they reached the bottom where we were; then jumped off, and straightaway seized her spade and fell to digging without a word. She was a pretty brunette of eighteen, strong and healthy; her clothes, even her coarse flannel trousers, were in good condition; and dirty as she was, she was women enough to stick a bunch of half ripe cherries in the side of her grimy bonnet!*

In the ealy 1860s, these women earned about 1s 2d per day – 6p – for their long hours of back-breaking work shifting coal, grading it, removing stones and a wide variety of other surface jobs.

Pit brow lasses were the last visible vestiges of an employment system which had made extensive use of child and female labour since the closing years of the eighteenth century. In those days women and children had been extensively used underground, not as miners, but to haul the trucks of coal from the face to the foot of the shafts.

As late as the early 1840s a government commission had been set up to investigate the use of child labour in pits, and the commission was apparently quite surprised to find, that while the use of children was less than they had expected, the use of women was extensive.

The reports of the commission led to the Coalmines Regulation Act of 1842, banning the use of children in the pits, and limiting the employment of women to jobs performed above rather than underground.

In 1865 a Parliamentary Select Committee sought to investigate the employment of women at the pit head – citing moral as well as physical grounds as to why such a practice might be outlawed. There was a strong Victorian lobby which disapproved of women wearing men's clothes and working in such a 'rough' environment. To counter accusations of lack of femininity, several Wigan pit girls were persuaded to be photographed by local Wigan professional photographers wearing first their working clothes, and again, in their 'Sunday best', to demonstrate how ladylike they could look! The committee left well alone! In 1880 another attempt was made to remove the women from the coal screens – they were by then predominantly employed in the moving of small coal trucks, the grading of coal, and in 'slack washing' (the cleaning of selected small coals for coke making) – and a deputation of local pit girls actually went to London and the House of Commons to present their case for being allowed to continue in their work. They continued to be an integral part of the Wigan mining scene well into this century.

*Coal pickers during the 1912 strike photographed on a Pemberton slag heap. Coal picking was not only restricted to times of strike. Orwell vividly describes whole crowds of people gathering coal from slag heaps during the Depression – when mine owners prosecuted a few people in order to protect their rights, but generally allowed the practice to go unheeded.*

When the Victoria Pit at Boars head was sunk in the closing years of the century, the shaft was still dug with pick and shovel. Indeed, many of the coalfaces in Wigan were still being worked – albeit on a larger scale – in much the same way as they had been worked a century before. As the century closed, all that was about to change. Electrical cutting equipment was introduced elsewhere in the Lancashire coalfield in the late 1890s, but as Wigan did not have a power station until the early years of this century, electricity was a little late in arriving. When it did, it greatly speeded up the cutting and extraction of the coal, and provided another market for it.

In Britain as a whole, the output of coal had risen from one hundred million tons annually in 1870 to two hundred and fifty million tons by the turn of the century – over twenty per cent of the total world output! Lancashire was producing some twenty-five million tons of the national output, and Wigan something approaching half of the Lancashire total from over a hundred pits.

The Maypole pit disaster on the evening of August 18th 1908 demonstrated to the town – if any reminder was necessary – the high price which had to be paid for coal, when seventy-five men lost their lives as a result of an underground explosion. When the bodies were found, some were still at their work places, overwhelmed by the fireball before they had had a chance to move. Another, a Methodist preacher, is said to have been found on his knees in prayer as he prepared to face the inevitable.

It was not the greatest disaster to hit the Lancashire coalfields, but it was the first to be widely reported in both words and pictures in the national press. Crowds were photographed as they waited at the

# The Maypole Disaster, 1908

 HE Maypole mining disaster of 1908 was the town's worst. A gas explosion deep underground killed seventy-five miners working setting charges in the pit. Only three men survived. The community at Abram was devastated by the disaster, which was reported widely and became front-page news on national as well as local papers. It was years before the last of the bodies were brought out of the pit – to be buried beneath a specially commissioned monument in Abram churchyard. The Maypole was the first mining disaster to be extensively reported through photographs, and it was one of the first in which breathing apparatus was used to help in the rescue. At the inquest and inquiry which followed, everybody blamed everybody else. Local mineowners claimed there was no gas in Wigan pits – a claim which every local miner knew to be a lie. Many recommendations were made but few were followed up. An almost identical disaster at Westhoughton in 1912 cost 334 lives and showed how little regard mineowners had taken of the advice which came out of the inquiry.

*Left: The Maypole – the ruins of the colliery headgear still stand in a small industrial estate.*
*Below: Several postcards were published to raise money for the bereaved families. In several of them, listed amongst the dead, were miners who had not been down the mine but who had removed their tallies from the pithead office to conceal their absenteeism! This fine fund-raising postcard was published in another important mining area, Barnsley, and shows the Yorkshire Rescue Party with (right) the breathing apparatus they used.*

Waiting for the News, Abram, near Wigan

Funeral of One of the Victims, Abram, near Wigan

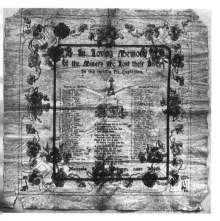

**Top:** *Waiting for News – crowds gathered at the pit head and in the surrounding fields within minutes of the explosion. The dust from the explosion turned all the local fields grey, and green footprints marked where relatives had run across the grass to the pit head.*

**Centre, left:** *Dundee postcard publisher James Valentine produced this illustration of the funeral of Thomas Pimblet on 24th August.*

**Centre, right:** *The Three survivors from the Maypole – Edward Farrell, William Doran and Richard Fairhurst – were working in a part of the mine which was shielded from the explosion and the fireball which roared through the underground roadways.*

**Left:** *Memorial Napkin – a printed napkin also produced to raise money for the bereaved, is a treasured possession in many local households over eighty years after the disaster.*

pithead for news; reporters from far and wide came to observe and record the village of Abram as it coped with the shock and the aftermath of a major disaster. For two days – long after they knew there was no hope – the crowds stood in the pit yard refusing to accept the obvious until it was clear that the three survivors rescued on the first night were the only ones to escape the underground holocaust.

*The Times* wrote a few days after the event:

> *Rain has fallen at intervals during the day, and the pit yard has presented a deserted appearance in striking contrast to the animated scenes which have been witnessed during the past two days. The combined effect of the downpour and the official announcement that there is no present hope of recovering further bodies has been that the patient crowd which has hitherto pressed around the police cordon have today remained indoors.*

Gas was *blamed* for the explosion, but the system whereby men did not get paid unless there was coal for them to shift was clearly *responsible* for the explosion. The shot firers went into the mine after the day shift was over to blast down the coal for the next shift to work. If they didn't do their job, the miners went short of pay – so pressure to fire was great, despite the fact that clear warnings had been given by government officials that there were atmospheric conditions prevailing which made an increase in underground gas a distinct possibility.

In the enquiry which followed, miners spoke frequently of gas and fires in Wigan mines. Maypole's manager – Arthur Rushton – who was actually just returning from holiday as the explosion occurred, told the enquiry:

> *There never was a colliery in the state in which they [the miners] say it was. It is most damnable the way they have talked about the colliery. I say the condition of the Maypole five minutes before the explosion took place did not warrant an explosion.*

But an explosion had taken place, and mining had claimed another batch of lives. The fires raged underground for weeks – during which time there were another series of explosions as more and more pockets of gas ignited. It would be years after the explosion that the last of the bodies were recovered.

Considering the number of mines in Wigan, the numbers of workers involved and the complexity of the underground workings, it is perhaps a considerable testament to the safety standards maintained underground that the Maypole was the most costly loss of life in one of the most heavily worked coalfields in the world.

Indeed, had it not been for the strict observance of procedures at the Maypole, many more lives might have been lost. The shot firers had only gone down the mine after the day shift had returned to the surface. It had once been common practice to drill and load charges before the miners were clear of the workings. That practice had been outlawed by regulations in the previous century. Several hundred miners had returned to the surface only an hour before the explosion.

Nevertheless, few lessons were learned from the disaster. While miners blamed management and the system under which they worked and were paid, management denied that there was gas, and tried to blame shoddy working practices. There was a strong suggestion that the shot firers had elected to use one large, rather than several small

*Engineers and fitters at Pemberton Colliery, around 1920. So extensive were the railway networks associated with the collieries that large railway staffs were required to keep them all running. The men are seen here posing on and in front of a 0–4–0 industrial locomotive.*

charges. There was a communication breakdown in that reports of gas the previous day were not acted upon. Above all, there was a system which made one worker answerable to his colleagues for their livelihood, and therefore put excessive pressure on the shot firers to disregard the risk and proceed with their firing. They were not able to answer the criticisms made of them at the subsequent inquest and inquiry. None of them had survived the explosion.

Although many recommendations were made, the lessons of Maypole were largely ignored – just a few years later an explosion at the Pretoria pit in nearby Westhoughton claimed over four times as many lives in very similar conditions.

Up until the First World War, the coal production graph continued to ascend, peaking at just under three hundred million tons nationally, with Wigan contributing considerably to that total.

By 1920, with some pits approaching four thousand feet deep, the intense working of the Wigan coalfield in the previous fifty to sixty years resulted in an increasing number of seams becoming either worked out, or too difficult to exploit any further. First of all faces were abandoned, then collieries, and by the time of nationalisation, there were just over twenty left working. As they too closed to leave only opencast workings and a privately owned drift mine, the great days of the Wigan coalfield passed into history for ever. The legacy, however – in terms of culture, tradition and the visible effects on the landscape – will be with us for many years to come.

Chapter Seven

# King Cotton

**At 5.30 am I was awoken by the tramp of the factory girls. My window
at the Royal Hotel looks upon the Market Place. I got up, and saw the
broad street busy with women and girls, all in clogshoon and most of
them with shawls on their heads, all tramping to work in groups of two
and three, and talking broad Lancashire audibly. Hundreds of them;
and hardly any men. The sun had not risen; it was dawn, and great
rosy clouds were in the sky. I went to bed again; and thought that
after all, my Hannah's life had been a harder and rougher, and a far
more humbling, life than that of these girls . . .**
Arthur Munby, diary entry, 11 September 1873

HE story of the cotton industry from the last quarter of
the eighteenth century is a story of the rapid trans-
formation of what had essentially been a cottage
industry for centuries into a major pioneer of mass
production. The rise of a few former spinners and
weavers to become the cotton barons of the town
started in the third quarter of the eighteenth century, stimulated by a
series of important innovations in the machinery upon which the
industry was based. As long as all the equipment involved in the
spinning of yarn and the weaving of cloth was manually operated,
cloth was a precious commodity, relatively high in price, especially if it
was coloured or patterned, and in relatively short supply. The advent
of mechanisation changed all that. In particular, the gradual
introduction of steam power to drive the machines revolutionised the
entire industry.

The first major steps towards automation were in the design and
operation of looms. Arguably the most important development of the
eighteenth century was the Jacquard loom, introduced in mainland
Europe as early as 1745, and itself a combination of ideas developed
from 1725 and 1728. It was the first major design change in hand-loom
weaving for over a century. With the Jacquard loom complex woven
patterns were possible without the need either for a team of workers or
complex manoeuvres.

The flying shuttle further speeded up the weaving process from 1733
when Robert Kay demonstrated his device for automating the back
and forth movement of the shuttle. A later invention in 1760 added
multiple shuttle boxes to looms, allowing multi-coloured cloths to be
produced more speedily.

Hargreaves' Spinning Jenny, invented in 1765 but not patented until

1770, was not the first machine designed to mechanise and speed up the spinning process. Paul's Spinning Machine of 1738 had attempted, none too successfully, to do the same thing. The spinning jenny was a hand-cranked machine that could spin sixteen or more threads at a time, and which was able, therefore, to do at least sixteen times as much work as the traditional spinning wheel. Arkwright's Throstle Frame (from the whistling thrush-like noise it made) and his later Water Frame – patented in 1769 and 1775 – were developments of Paul's machine for the spinning of cotton yarns.

The greatest advance, however, came with the combination of those earlier ideas into Crompton's Mule, patented in 1779 and so named because it was a hybrid machine which used the best of Paul's and Hargreaves' ideas. It revolutionised the spinning process, and it proved to be so successful that mule spinning was to be the mainstay of the great spinning mills for much of the nineteenth century, despite the fact that the faster and more efficient ring spindle was invented in America as early as 1828.

Together, these inventions led to a range of developments that greatly increased the amount of spun yarn available to the growing number of factories and weaving mills in the area.

The men, women and children who operated these machines earned a pittance for their twelve- and fourteen-hour days. In the second half of the eighteenth century, the average local wage for a six-day week varied from two to five shillings (10p – 25p). Skilled men earned the highest, semi-skilled women the lowest. As the workforce was predominantly women in the spinning mills, the average wage would have been near to two, rather than five, shillings for a total of up to eighty four hours. Girls from as young as six years of age also worked in the spinning mills, starting at a shilling a week rising to one shilling and sixpence by the time they were twelve! The average earnings of a

*Eighteenth-century handloom weavers' cottages, Wigan Lane. The bottom floor of the building, which was partly underground, contained the weaving shop, where the handloom weaver worked – in order to keep the yarn pliable while it was being woven, and to stop it breaking, conditions had to be kept damp*

weaver at the same time varied from six to eight shillings a week (30p – 40p). Women earned about a shilling less, and children could expect to earn two shillings – 10p! Many of the handloom weavers were employed, usually by middlemen or millowners, even though they continued to work at home. Their employer would provide the loom (or subsidise the cost) and they would work only for him. Others were effectively self-employed and paid by the total number of 'pieces' they wove in a week – the original piece work.

*Eckersley's Swan Meadow Mills – a vast complex which developed over a century and more. Until 1988 cotton weaving continued on this site, albeit in a single shed towards the end.*

Wigan, in fact, was relatively slow to introduce powered spinning. Although spinning machines were in widespread use in much of Lancashire from the 1770s and 1780s, Wigan's lack of sufficient fast-flowing streams hindered their introduction until the introduction of steam power some years later. Boulton & Watt's first viable industrial steam engine was installed in Drinkwater's Spinning Mill in Manchester in 1789, but it took some time for the novelty of steam power to be accepted as commercially viable by the mill owners. The first steam driven spinning mills in Wigan were opened some time around the year 1810.

In 1816, trade directory entries still show a predominance of home-based industry rather than 'manufactories'. Fifty 'Cotton Manu-facturers' are listed in 1816 directories, along with seventeen 'Linen & Check Manufacturers', six 'Fustian Manufacturers', four sizers, nine dyers and three shuttle makers (fustian was a hybrid cloth with a linen warp and a cotton weft). With the exception of sixteen, all are listed as individuals rather than companies, with private addresses rather than mills.

This compares with the situation in 1838, when thirty-nine

companies are listed, with a workforce of over six and a half thousand. In that intervening period mechanisation had arrived. The first spinning mills had been mechanised about 1810 and by 1825 over thirty steam engines were at work. By 1838, that figure had passed the one hundred and twenty mark. In the early 1820s William Woods introduced the town's first power looms into Trencherfield Mill.

The first decades of the nineteenth century had seen the most dramatic changes to the industry – changes which had not always been welcomed and which had brought with them considerable hardship and not a little turmoil. Power looms were introduced steadily and the cost savings that they brought dramatically reduced the price of a length of cloth and effectively made handloom weavers uneconomic.

Many continued to struggle on, amid declining wages for ever longer working hours, and in the face of the mounting and irreversible challenge of the powerloom. It was also a matter of grievance and regret that the new powerlooms could be operated by partially skilled workers rather than experienced craftsmen. As wages fell, many families were thrown into considerable poverty. This led to a county-wide strike of weavers in 1808 to fight for higher wages, and in Wigan strikers attacked the homes of non-strikers and removed the shuttles from their looms in an effort to stop them working.

At a time of rising costs and falling wages, the problems continued for decades and a second campaign – this time not only over wages but also against highly priced basic foodstuffs – took place in 1829. A period of machine wrecking led William Woods to borrow two cannon from Haigh Hall and position them strategically covering the approaches to Trencherfield! At that time, it is estimated that something like five or six thousand handloom weavers were at work in the town, most of them in their own homes. Three companies effectively controlled the livelihoods of all those people – Eckersleys, Rylands and Woods. There were other smaller operations, but the big three provided most of the weavers' yarns, and therefore controlled their working lives.

Adding the number of people employed in spinning, the town actually offered employment to fewer people in the textile industry in the late 1830s than it had in the early 1820s, although over the same period output had increased almost tenfold! The pattern of employment had changed considerably in the interval, however. Of the seven thousand or so people employed in the textile industry in the early 1820s, less than a thousand worked in factories: the remainder were all based at home. By the late 1830s, however, over five thousand out of a total workforce of six and a half thousand were working in mills. There were, according to factory inspectors' reports, twenty-one mills working in the town by 1835.

The population of Wigan parish at that time – and it can be assumed that virtually all the employees lived within the parish if not within the town – was 44,500, so the textile industry accounted for something like 25% of the working population.

In the early days, woollen fabrics had been produced in quantity in Wigan, along with linen. Cotton was a relatively late arrival. In the early-nineteenth century, however, cotton was in the ascendancy. There were still some linen manufacturers working in the 1820s, but over the next thirty years their trade virtually died out. The same pattern had affected the woollen industry in the previous century, and the first half of the nineteenth century also saw the end of fustian production.

The great mills which still dominate the town's skyline started to appear during the first half of the nineteenth century – or at least the first mills to stand on these sites did. In many cases, the present buildings are the second or even third to be built in the space of less than a century as the size of operations, and the sophistication of machinery accelerated.

William Woods built his Sovereign Mills at the beginning of the century, and the first Trencherfild Mill about 1820, the present mill being the third on that site. By 1822, the first Swan Meadow Mill was in operation – although a fraction of the size of the huge rambling complex which exists today.

Victoria Mill was opened by Thomas Taylor in the mid-1830s but, unlike the others, no longer dominates the lower end of Wallgate. A magnificent painting of lunchtime at Taylor's Mill, now in the Manchester City Art Gallery, does, however, give us a vivid impression of what it once looked like.

This massive expansion programme in mill building had the effect of taking the total workforce up to and well beyond the figure employed before mechanisation. By 1860, the total number of people employed in the industry had exceeded nine thousand. Output had increased eight times in the county as a whole, and Lancashire was producing 2,000,000,000 yards of cotton a year! Two years later depression hit the county. Wigan was not spared its effects.

*The invoice for the building of Rylands' Gidlow Mill, April 1868, showing a grand total of nearly £141,000.*

The cotton industry was by that time highly dependent upon American cotton. In earlier days the supply had come from a number of countries, most notably Egypt and India, but American production was on such a scale by the end of the eighteenth century that it outstripped all other producing countries. The growth of Liverpool, and the enormous shipping trade between America and the port, made American cotton almost the exclusive raw material of the Lancashire cotton towns.

Liverpool had received less than a thousand ships in 1750, a figure that had grown to 4,500 by 1800. By 1840 sixteen thousand ships a year were docking at the port, with the quantity of cotton imported rising from 10,000 bales in 1750 to nearly 100,000 by 1800 and over two million by 1850. Into Liverpool in 1833, for instance, £15m worth of cotton was shipped, while the port exported £12m-worth.

With such a dependence on a single source of supply, any problems in America were going to ripple over to Liverpool, Wigan, Manchester and the other Lancashire cotton towns very quickly. The American Civil War was just such an event, and by 1862 seven thousand of the town's nine thousand textile workers were laid off, with only two of the town's thiry-five mills working. That situation persisted for the duration of the war, but the recovery was just as dramatic as the slump had been. Almost as soon as hostilities ceased on the other side of the

*Inside Eckersley's Mills in the 1920s.*

*The Dorma weaving shed – seen here in 1986 when it was the last and working shed in Wigan. There were one hundred and eighty looms controlled by a dozen weavers. While modern health and safety legislation required weavers to wear ear protection, no such luxury was afforded to the vast workforce in cotton's heyday. Amidst the deafening noise of the weaving shed lipreading was commonplace.*

Atlantic, Wigan millowners braced themselves for the return of a steady supply of raw material, and in some cases built splendid new and entirely modern mills to meet the expected demand.

One-time handloom weaver, Joseph Rylands with his two sons had set up smaller weaving businesses in St. Helens and in Wallgate, before building the Gidlow Mills complex at the top of Mesnes Park. Despite the fact that the American Civil War was still in full flow, planning for the new mill had started in 1865, although building did not commence until 1866 or early 1867. The buildings were completed by the end of 1867 and equipped early in 1868. The entire mill was built and equipped for a total of £140,000. It is interesting to note that it is now costing in excess of twenty times that amount to refurbish it as part of Wigan College of Technology, one hundred and twenty-five years later!

By 1869 the local directories show that Woods – after building larger mills at Trencherfield – had sold Sovereign Mills to Lamb & Moore, a leading local colliery owner. Thus they supplied coal from their own mines to power their mills! (It was the elevated gantry from Lamb & Moore's Meadow pit to Newtown which so interested George Formby Snr. and became the legendary Wigan Pier of the comedian's music hall jokes.)

Many of the big new mills were predominantly spinning mills – Swan Meadow, Newhall, Britannia, Low, Ellesmere, Bradford Place, Rose Bridge, Victoria, Sovereign, May, Chapel Lane, Trencherfield and others. Other, related enterprises also grew up. In Millgate and Harrogate Street, dyeworks had been established. There were bobbin turners in Queen Street and at least two spindle and fly makers in Scholes. Dyeing had been concentrated in the Millgate area at least since the beginning of the century, while, at the same time, Scholes had several shuttle makers. There was also a considerable trade with the bobbin mills of both the Lake District and the Blackburn area.

Without doubt, the bias in Wigan's textile workforce had shifted over the first seventy years of the nineteenth century. In 1800 it had been predominantly made up of weavers – weaving at that time being a slow labour-intensive industry based at home. By 1870 the bias was clearly towards employment in the spinning mills, with only a relatively small proportion of the total workforce weaving.

Considering that ring spinning had been in use in America since the 1830s, it is surprising to note that it was the late 1870s before the first Wigan mill converted to the faster and much more space efficient system. When ring spinning was eventually introduced on a large scale into Wigan in the 1880s, the number of working spindles in the town increased dramatically until, early this century, there were over one million.

Considering that in the 1850s, the total number of working spindles had probably not yet reached 50,000, that was a dramatic increase indeed. When the third Trencherfield Mill was opened in 1908, it alone had 84,000 – retaining 24,000 of the mule spindles and introducing 60,000 rings. Eckersley's Swan Meadow Mills complex – really six mills on the same site – boasted a quarter of a million spindles on its own!

In the 1870s clothing factories also opened in the town – the most

*Coops factory in Dorning Street was opened in 1872. Timothy Coop's business had grown from a one-man operation in the early-1860s. Later in the century, the size of the factory was doubled.*

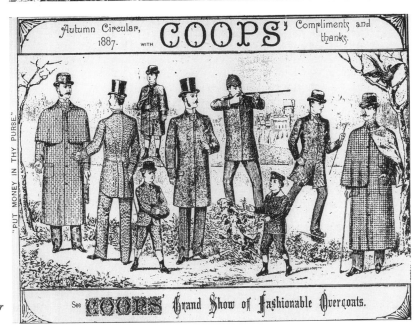

*All the rage in 1887 – an advertisement for Coops' autumn range of smart outdoor wear for gentlemen.*

important being Timothy Coop's and, along with others, provided an additional source of employment. By the outbreak of the Great War, the workforce was eight thousand – one thousand less than its peak in the 1860s, but output was higher than ever. The workforce rose dramatically between the two world wars to a peak of nearly eleven thousand, but by the 1920s, some of the smaller mills were already closing in the face of strong overseas competition.

1908 can really be seen as the end of an era for the textile industry in Wigan – although it by no means represented a turning point in the industry's fortunes. It was, however, the date at which the last mill built

# The Cotton Mills

**W**IGAN's last cotton weaving shed closed only very recently, bringing to an end a tradition that goes back to the fourteenth century. For women, the coal screen and the cotton mills were the two major places of employment.

Wigan once had dozens of working mills, taking advantage of the damp conditions, the good network of canal and rail transport, and a large and willing workforce. The nineteenth century saw a major expansion of the industry, with spinning and weaving moving out of cellars and lofts in houses into large manufactories. Cotton once accounted for over fifty per cent of the employment in the town. The production statistics were enormous – over one million spindles were working in Wigan's spinning mills in the first quarter of this century. The town offered employment across a wide spectrum of textile trades – spinning, weaving – both in factories and on handlooms at home – and in ready-made clothing. At its peak, the textile industry employed over ten thousand people in the town, over three-quarters of them women.

WIGAN MILL GIRLS, WEAVING-ROOM, N° 2.

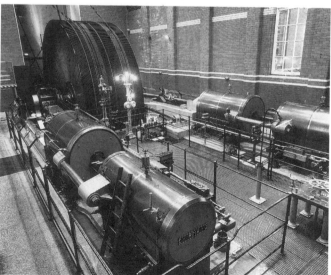

*Above, left: Weaving Room Rylands Mill – one of an extensive series of postcards celebrating the textile industry in the town at the turn of the century. Rylands Mill is now a major site of Wigan College of Technology, renamed as the Pagefield Building.*
*Above, right: Wigan Mill Girls c1910 – the uniforms are typical of those worn by over seven thousand workers in over fifty mills.*
*Left: Trencherfield Mill Engine – this huge twin engine once powered Trencherfield Mill. The mill closed twenty years ago as a spinning mill, although the engine now runs for the benefit of tourists.*

*Right:* Mill hands at Eckersleys Swan Meadow Mills queuing for tea in 1942.
*Centre:* Dorma Weaving Shed, 1986 – this was the last weaving shed in Wigan, producing 4½ million metres of cotton a year. It has now closed.
*Bottom, left:* Drawing frames, Rylands Mill – the workforce posed proudly for the turn-of-the-century camera.
*Bottom, right:* Trencherfield Mill – built by a canal rather than a railway, it preserved an old tradition. The third mill on the site, it was the largest spinning mill in Wigan.

DRAWING FRAMES.

by the side of a canal was opened – the third Trencherfield Mill. It is probably true to say that had the previous two mills not occupied the same canalside site, the third mill might have been built elsewhere. The days when the canal bank was the logical place to site a large mill were long gone.

As long ago as the early 1860s, May Mill in Pemberton had been built, not alongside the Leeds and Liverpool Canal, but adjacent to the most successful colliery complex in the area – Blundell's Pemberton Colliery. With its direct rail access through the colliery sidings, it had everything a modern mill could need – and more. The sidings provided easy loading of finished products, unloading and storage of raw materials, and a fast route to the rest of the country. By special arrangement with Blundells, May Mills' steam engines were powered by Pemberton coal, shipped straight from the pit head to the furnaces, and at pit head prices, representing a considerable cost saving to the mill's owners.

In 1868, Rylands had also seen the future of railways as far as the carriage of both raw materials and finished cloth was concerned. Gidlow Mill, built alongside the main London to Preston railway, had its own sidings and its own goods yards; such mills were the shape of things to come. The canal may have still had many decades of useful life ahead of it for the slow carriage of large quantities of coal, but in the days of fiercer competition, and greater demand for textiles, the rapid movement possible by rail was essential.

*Pemberton Colliery goods yards gave direct rail access to May Mills – a vast improvement on a canalside location.*

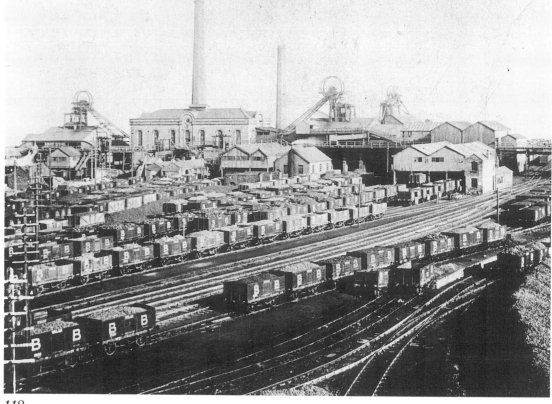

Chapter Eight

# The Victorian Town

**They did not look like women, or at least a stranger new to the district might easily have been misled by their appearance, as they stood together in a group by the pit's mouth. There were about a dozen of them there – all 'pit girls' as they were called; women who wore a dress more than half masculine, and who talked loudly and laughed discordantly, and some of whom, God knows, had faces as hard and brutal as the hardest of their collier brothers and husbands and sweethearts. They had lived among the coal pits, and had worked early and late at the 'mouth' ever since they had been old enough to take part in the heavy labour. It was not to be wondered at that they had lost all bloom of womanly modesty and gentleness. Their mothers had been 'pit girls' in their time, their grandmothers in theirs; they had been born in coarse homes; they had fared hardly, and worked hard, they had breathed in the dust and grime of coal, and somehow or other, it seemed to stick to them and reveal itself in their natures as it did in their bold unwashed faces . . .**
**. . . Riggan [Wigan] was a crooked rambling cross-grained little place. From one wide street with its jumble of old tumble-down shops, and glaring new ones, branched out narrow up-hill or down-hill thoroughfares, edged by the colliers houses, with an occasional tiny provision shop, where bread and bacon ranged alongside flabby cabbages . . .**
Francis Hodgson Burnett, *That Lass O' Lowrie's* (1877)

 HE rate of expansion of the town in the first half of the nineteenth century was considerable. The population of the borough trebled between 1800 and 1850 – from ten thousand to thirty thousand – while the parish population had reached about 77,000. Ten years later the figures were 38,000 in the borough and just under 95,000 for the parish. The area covered by the parish was, however, much less rural than it had been at the turn of the century. Many of the once small and separate villages had grown to merge with the town, making a large and heavily industrialised conurbation. Whereas in 1800 a large proportion of those living outside the borough but still within the parish limits had been employed on the land, this was no longer the case by 1850. That reflected a general movement of labour into factories where work was abundant, even if living conditions in the town were often appalling.

Whilst many aspects of Wigan life had changed dramatically, some

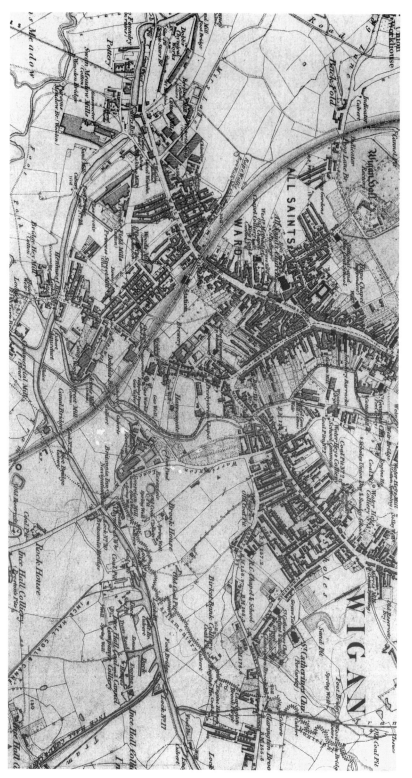

A section of the first Ordnance Survey map of Wigan, dating from the 1840s. It is instructive to compare this map with the 1827 map reproduced on page 74. Immediately evident is the railway, carving its way through the centre of the town. Paradoxically, however, the canal, seen here along the bottom of the map, was entering its most successful period, with record amounts of coal and merchandise being carried, especially westwards to Liverpool. Note the several tramways that serve the canal, including those of the Ince Hall Coal and Cannel Company. The tramroad that ended at 'Wigan Pier' can be seen running down to the canal in the south-west corner of the map. Note, also, the increasing number of schools, mills, churches . . . and houses.

things had hardly changed at all. The 1685 charter granted by King James II, which established the pattern of local government, had laid down that the Corporation should comprise thirty men – twelve aldermen, of whom two should be elected mayor and recorder, and eighteen 'capital burgesses' or councillors. By the Corporation Act of 1835, nothing had changed. The council still had an identical structure. Also unchanged was the lack of representation of most of the townsfolk – there were still only 667 'qualified householders' entitled to vote in council elections! To qualify for a vote, a householder had to own his own house and have an income exceeding ten pounds *per annum*. The qualification for local elections was slightly less stringent than for parliamentary ones. Only about six hundred householders were qualified to vote in parliamentary elections, together with the burgesses who all had an additional vote by virtue of their position!

By the mid 1860s, the number of voters was still less than one thousand. By 1870, however, the franchise was extended to include nearly four and a half thousand voters, and the size of the council increased – reflecting the continued growth of the town – to twelve aldermen and thirty councillors.

Electorally, the town was divided into five wards – All Saints, Queen Street, Scholes, Swinley and St. George's – each electing six councillors. The mayor, recorder and ten aldermen were, after the 1835 Act, still elected by the councillors from their own number, just as they had been for two centuries.

By 1835 the town held three courts – weekly petty sessions, quarter sessions and a court of record, and by 1835 enjoyed the protection of a police force which cost the local authority £538 in that year.

One thing that definitely had changed was the relationship between church and town. In the seventeenth century the parish church had stood alone in Wigan, and the only available choice was whether to attend or not to attend. By 1835 there was a total of nine Episcopal churches and chapels in the parish. In addition to All Saints, the eight others – all called chapels, as only the parish church was known by the loftier title in nineteenth-century Wigan – included St. George's, built in 1781, and Scholes Chapel within the borough boundaries, the remainder being in the outlying villages and districts. There were also six Catholic chapels – one of them, St. John's, having recently been built at a cost of £8,000 – four Wesleyan, four Independent, two Baptist, two Unitarian, one Presbyterian, one Independent Methodist, and one Swedenborgian, otherwise known as 'New Church', its followers adhering to the doctrines of Swedish philosopher, Emmanuel Swedenborg, who had established his Church in the eighteenth century. In this century it became known as the New Jerusalem Church.

That was a total of thirty places of worship for a population of 45,000, or one church for every fifteen hundred people! By contrast, given the range and number of churches in the town, and the number of their adherents who shunned drink, the number of places in which beer was sold was remarkable! There were one hundred and forty three hotels, inns and public houses in the 1860s in the borough alone – twice that many if the outlying districts were included. In addition, there were three hundred licensed beer sellers! The beer sellers usually sold from their houses, the local people bringing jugs, buckets, glasses or whatever other receptacle they wished, and buying direct from the back door. Given the living and working conditions so many of them had to endure, seeking solace in a pint is perhaps hardly surprising. The 1860s were, after all, uncertain times for the town's workforce.

In the previous chapter, reference was made to the problems created by the American Civil war as far as the town's economy was concerned. J. Worrall, writing in 1869, said of the cotton industry that

*Watchmaking continued to be well represented in the town in the nineteenth century. The watch at the top is by Holt and dates from 1851. The one at the bottom was made by Archibald Coates in about 1750. Several watchmakers had premises in Standishgate – the town's premier shopping street in the 1870s.*

> *The proximity of Liverpool, and the facilities for carriage naturally brought a portion of the cotton trade to Wigan, where it has flourished to a considerable extent, there being several mills of the very largest size, and though at present with all other trades somewhat depressed, it is hoped that it will again attain at least its former prosperity. The trade was totally stopped during the recent American War, when the populace manifested exemplary patience under very trying circumstances, which, however, were greatly relieved by the magnificent contributions sent from all parts of the world to Lancashire, and which were liberally distributed by a local committee . . . During the cotton famine, the streets of the town were greatly improved, paving and sewering being done to a large extent, and new roads were laid out by the otherwise unemployed mill hands. A portion of the funds remaining in the hands of the Lord Mayor of London has been allotted to the building of an infirmary, and other liberal contributions having been made, a suitable building for this purpose will now soon be erected.*

Millowners had played their part to the full in trying to ameliorate the effects of the Cotton Famine on their workforce, with Woods and Eckersleys alone spending as much as £3,500 per week between them on supplying bread and soup to those they had had to lay off. Although unrecorded, other millowners probably did the same. It is interesting to note, however, that the local authority had also made good use of the sudden availability of a large workforce to improve civic amenities.

It has already been noted that by the middle of the nineteenth century something over half the workforce was employed either in mining or in textiles. The remainder were employed in a wide range of trades, crafts and professions.

Since the early-eighteenth century, Wigan had become something of a centre for the design and manufacture of clocks and watches – some of them very delicate and highly ornamented. By 1870 there were no fewer than twenty-four watch and clock makers working in the town, many of them in Wallgate and Standishgate.

Clock and watch making was one of the few of the earlier crafts to survive in the town. By 1870 there were no pewter makers, no potters, and few handloom weavers left. Jobs were concentrated in the large factories and mills, some of which, like the Kirkless Hall Company established in 1858, would have a major impact on employment in the years to come. Out of the small plant grew the Wigan Coal and Iron Company which later employed an enormous workforce.

Wigan had also become a major shopping centre – and with a growing population to serve, the number and variety of shops was considerable. The town centre was a very different place than it is today, quite apart from the major current redevelopment to create the Galleries and Marketgate shopping centres. Standishgate, now dominated by a few large stores, was once a street of many small shops selling a very wide variety of goods.

Enough is known about the town in 1870 to be able to reconstruct a walk down Standishgate on either side of the street and to get a real flavour of the range and variety of shops it contained. Walking today from John Menzies to Bryan House, there are perhaps a dozen shops. A century and a quarter ago there were forty.

The John Menzies site was the Royal Hotel and, where Burtons now stands, there was Walter Wilding, tobacconist, with the offices of Maskell Peace, the town clerk, above, John Pendlebury, milliner and dressmaker, and Thomas Gledhill, tailor, with James Bibby's law office above. Continuing down the street, the Victorian shopper would come next to Pearson's bookshop – they were stationers and printers as well – with another solicitor, Thomas Taylor, above. Next was Johnson Grounds, watchmakers, and John Hare's grocery shop. Nos. 17 and 19 were owned by William Birkett, hatter and draper, with next door to that, at No. 21, Thomas Dugdale, one of the town's first photographers who also ran the Green Man public house at No. 130. At No. 23 was J. C. Leach, upholsterer, check and gingham maker, with Richard Hardy's chemist's shop at No. 25. Another tailor, Elijah Hardy, was at No. 27, with Hill & Cordeaux, butchers, next door.

Thomas Dawson's tailors shop at No. 31 had a surveyor, Isaac Perrins, above, and was next door to Charles Irvine, boot and shoe maker. Robert Douglas's drapery occupied 35-37 Standishgate, with another solicitor, Edward Scott, using the upstairs of No. 35.

At No. 39 was a saddle and harness marker, William Jardine, and Nos. 41-43 housed William Platt's grocery, with warehouses behind as he was also a tea dealer and corn merchant. Another grocery was next door, owned by William Altham, with John Sweetman's chemist shop at No. 49. Yet another tea dealer and grocer – Robert Beasley – was at No. 51 with Copkand's drapery at No. 53. Edward Lowe, grocer, was at No. 59. Between the White Horse and the Dog I'Thatch was a leather dealer, R. & W. Proctor, and Robert Winstanley, surgeon!

The other side of the street was just as varied – Richard Platt was at the top of the street, a music dealer, musical instrument seller, insurance agent and printer. Barton's tailor shop was next door, with Mary Brown, grocer, at No. 8. Also at No. 8 was J. H. Coke, veterinary surgeon, and at No. 10 was Joseph Hurst, confectioner. No. 12 was Pender's dress shop, Pollard's hat shop was at No. 14 and Jonathan Hallam, wine and spirit merchant was at No. 16. Additionally, there

# Education

FROM a situation in the early years of the last century when many children never went to school – their parents requiring them to work to help the family survive – nineteenth-century legislation soon made it compulsory for all children to get at least a rudimentary education. Wigan's education system developed rapidly in the last century to one of which the town was rightly proud. At primary and secondary level, good schools and teachers became the rule rather than the exception, although by today's standards the education was basic and the discipline somewhat harsh. Children being caned for relatively mild offences fitted in with the Victorian belief that if they were beaten hard enough and often enough, all children would eventually conform. The Bluecoat School was one of the earliest in the town, and a frequently photographed establishment from the earliest days of the camera. In further education, the establishment of classes for the education of miners dates back to the middle of the last century. The Mining School followed very shortly – one of the first in the country, as was the Art School founded in the 1850s.

*Left: Music Tuition – there is a strong tradition of music education in the town. This picture of about 1895 shows a rather informal appreciation of music by four youngsters!*
*Below: The girls of the Convent in Standish-gate dressed in their Sunday best to meet King George V in 1913. Cyril Foley took this splendid photograph outside the now demolished Convent and Will Smith of Wigan Lane sold several hundred postcard copies of it.*
*Opposite, top: Bluecoat National School Class c1875 – Group 4 pose for their school picture – the boys with the holes in their jerseys got in the front row even then!*
*Opposite, bottom: British Empire Tableau – a Pemberton school's tribute to mark the coronation of King George V in 1902.*

# Pubs

 IT has often been said that northern towns had a pub on every corner. While that may be a bit of an overstatement, it is not far short of the mark. There were a great many more pubs in Wigan at the turn of the century than in many other towns. Even recently, until redevelopment thinned them out a bit, trying to have a drink in every pub on Standishgate and Wigan Lane was considered a near-suicidal challenge! There is no doubt that the two major sources of employment in the town – the mines and the mills – both created a thirst, and having a pint or two on the way home from work to clear the dust of the mines and the fluff of the mills out of mouth and throat was a fairly standard practice, much-loved by the men and heavily criticised by wives trying to make ends meet on slender pay packet and by Victorian moralists. Many of the best-known pubs in the town have been demolished in the last twenty years – the Legs of Man – both top and bottom legs – and the Commercial went when the Wigan Centre was built in the 1970s. The Park went to make way for the Galleries shopping precinct, and the site of the Saracens Head is now somewhere in the middle of the carriageway of the new ring road. Others seen in these pictures went long ago.

*Left: The Queens Head once stood in Market Place and was demolished in the closing years of the last century. Next door are the premises of W. Barnes, Whitesmith, Bellhanger and Gas Fitter.*

*Bottom, left: The White Lion, Market Street – another pub demolished to make way for the redevelopment of Wigan's best shopping street.*

*Below: The Coach & Horses, Hallgate. Taken about 1880 this pub was demolished just a couple of years later. It had been on this site for almost two hundred years, being known as the Pied Bull until about 1815.*

*The Harp Inn, Scholes – like many, this one actually was on a street corner. The picture was taken on May 8th 1901 and shows a group of local councillors posing with landlord Robert Richards.*

were hairdressers, perfumers (the chosen Victorian spelling), insurance agents, white-smiths and ironmongers, shoe and boot makers, another vet, William Woods at No. 26, while a surgeon at No. 28 was strategically placed next door to a barber at 30! The chief magistrate to the borough, Thomas Heald, was at No. 38, and John Hargreaves, watchmaker, at 40 – all in all, a varied range of shops for our Victorian predecessors to consider.

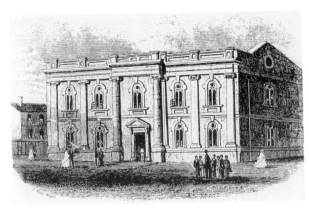

In education, great advances had been made. In the eighteenth century only two properly constituted schools had existed – the Grammar School, and the Bluecoat & National, opened in 1774 with twenty pupils who were clothed and educated free. Haigh and Upholland had had church schools since the seventeenth century, and Pemberton since 1878. By the mid-nineteenth century, the town had, in addition to church schools, 31 other schools where education varying from very good to very rudimentary could be received. Some of these were run privately; others were National Schools. In addition, five thousand children attended fifteen Sunday schools each week.

*The Old Grammar School – one of several sites in the town before the buildings on Mesnes Road were built in this century.*

Thomas Taylor MA was in charge of the Grammar School in Rodney Street, with John Young BA as his second master. Among the other schools, the Misses Brown ran a private school for young ladies in Dicconson Street – a few doors away from the Wesleyan School –

*Manor House School.*

*The 'New Town Hall' in Market Place, complete with butchers' shops, in this late-nineteenth-century photograph taken shortly before its demolition.*

and Miss Catherine McEwan ran a day school at No. 85 Standishgate in premises shared with W. S. Masters & Sons, general agents.

As far as civic buildings were concerned, there was the town hall, built in 1720 in the Market Place. It was a curious building, with civic offices in the upper floor, but the main street frontage in the 1870s – from Nos. 14 to 26 Market Place – entirely occupied by seven butchers' shops. Messrs Hall, Bibby, Benson (pork butcher), Haworth, Holcroft, Mrs Cowell at No. 24, and Woods at No. 26, carrying on their business downstairs must have at times given the councillors some rather less than fragrant air to breath while going about their civic debates!

There was a public hall in King Street which had been built in 1816, and the Moot Hall in the Market Place – rebuilt in 1829 and demolished in early 1870 to make way for road improvements. The town hall was demolished in 1882 when the new building in Rodney Street was opened. Additionally, the town had a theatre, a savings bank which had been opened in King Street in 1821, and could boast having had a subscription library since 1787, a waterworks since 1761 and gasworks since 1823.

The first half of the Victorian era saw an unprecedented expansion in the amount of workers' housing in the town – much of it small and with houses closely packed together, but clean and functional. Huge terraces of houses were built, providing homes for thousands, and work for many more. The town supported nineteen brickmakers by 1870, a number of bricklayers, and over forty builders and joiners, and

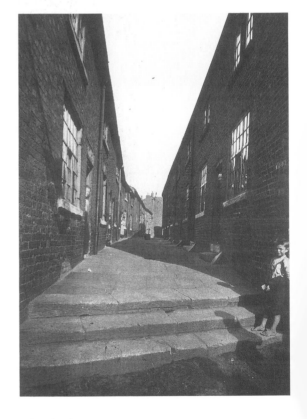

*Eighteenth- and early-nineteenth century housing survived in a number of small closes and yards off Standishgate (the area in the bottom photograph was known as Little London) until major redevelopment at the end of the last century and the early years of the present, and elsewhere in the town until the years just before the Second World War. Of this type of one-up, one-down cottage, George Orwell in* The Road to Wigan Pier *noted 'walls coming apart and water comes in . . . landlord bad, rent 4s, rates 2s 3d . . . Corporation are trying to evict them for overcrowding, but cannot find other houses to send them to'.*

nearly as many plumbers and glaziers.

Four building societies were already in operation – the Wigan Permanent Benefit, the Wigan Provident Benefit, the Kirkless Benefit and the Queens Investment & Building Society of Manchester. One was in Standishgate and one in Market Place; the other two were in King Street, where there are still building societies today. The most popular site for today's building societies – Library Street – did not exist in 1870, having been developed in the early 1890s.

In 1889, the Borough of Wigan became a county borough – administratively independent of the recently created Lancashire County Council, although Wigan had already been relatively independent for a long time. County borough status, however, gave the local authority the powers it needed to direct Wigan's development into the twentieth century without having to take account of an unnecessary amount of external red tape.

Parallel to the development of the town as a shopping centre were the creation and growth of a public transport system that could convey shoppers and workers into, out of and around the town. By the early years of the nineteenth century, several 'omnibus' companies had sprung up, offering regular horse-drawn passenger services from some of the outlying districts. Typical of these was the Wigan and Haigh Omnibus

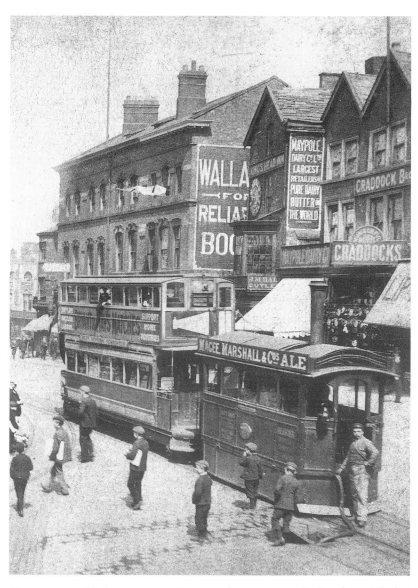

*A steam tram taking on water in Market Place.*

Company, which ran several return journeys each day into Market Place from Haigh and Aspull. Similar companies operated omnibus services from Pemberton, Standish and elsewhere. Over rough stone or, at best, cobbled roads and streets, however, passenger comfort must have been very poor indeed.

The first trams in the town arrived in the early 1880s, plans having been agreed in 1878 and 1879. For a variety of reasons – the most often quoted being that the streets of Wigan were too narrow for standard gauge rails, the first tramways used a narrow gauge 3'6" track, and the first lines, consisting of six miles of track, were authorised between Lamberhead Green and Market Place, between Market Place and Leyland Mill Lane and between Rodney Street and Bridge Street in Hindley. For some reason, the Hindley Line was not designed to connect with the rest of the system!

First to be built was the Lamberhead Green Line, and the official opening took place on 31st July 1880, with passenger traffic starting on the following Monday. The link between Wallgate and Market Place at the end of the Lamberhead Green line was not ready in time, however, and did not open for a further month. These were horse-drawn trams, of course, but, with the vehicle running on rails, the comfort of the trip into Wigan was substantially improved. Rails also eased the movement of vehicles – meaning that a horse could pull a much heavier load on a tram than it had been able to do with an omnibus. The steep pull up Wallgate, however, still posed a major problem.

As the tramcars themselves had a definite front and back – the staircase had to be at the back – they were designed so that the whole body could be swung round on the chassis at either end of the line so that it, too, always faced the right way! The horse got no rest at the terminus, for it had the job of pulling the heavy car round on its chassis.

By November 1881, a Wilkinson steam locomotive, built at Pemberton, was under trial on the line, and steam was introduced officially for passenger services by the autumn of 1882. In order to exploit steam, the system had to be modified. Water supplies had to be laid on at the termini, turning triangles or loop tracks had to be laid to permit the locomotive either to run round the passenger car – where newly-designed, double-ended cars were in use – or to permit the whole combination to be turned round. As the steam engines were only permitted to pull, they always had to be facing the way the tram was going. Additionally, as they could not run in reverse, the loop tracks had to be able to turn the locomotive round rather than just simply allowing it to connect to the other end of the tram.

The original introduction of steam, however, was short lived, and the horse-drawn trams were back in service for a time in 1894 – with only a limited service as the company had already sold most of its horses! Steam returned later in the same year with improved locomotives, and the service improved considerably.

By the end of the century, there were lines to Hindley, Platt Bridge and Martland Mill, but the line to Leyland Mill Lane up Wigan Lane, authorised in the first Tramway Order, had never been built. The original company, the Wigan Tramways Company Ltd., survived only a few years and went into receivership in 1890, being replaced by the Wigan and District Tramways Company Ltd., but that too was a short-lived enterprise. As the century drew to a close, Wigan Corporation Tramways came into existence, and plans were drawn up for a major expansion of the system.

The Corporation and local businessmen met in 1899 for the first time to discuss what was perhaps the greatest single step forward for the town since the building of the gas works in 1823 – the building of an electricity generating station in Bradford Place by the banks of the canal. Wigan was about to get the dual benefits of electric lights and electric trams.

Orders for the overhead cabling for the new electric trams, for new rails and for the host of other pieces of equipment necessary, were placed before the end of the century – surprisingly not with local firms despite the strong industrial background the town had.

The first electric cars, like their horse-drawn and steam-hauled predecessors, were built to the narrow-gauge specification. It would not be until 1903 that the standard gauge was adopted, and all Wigan tram lines had to be re-laid.

The real expansion of the system took place in the first decade of the twentieth century, but as the nineteenth century came to a close, the west, east and south sides of the town were relatively well catered for in a way that the railways.had never managed to do. Despite the network of railway lines surrounding the town, and three stations in the centre, there was no real suburban rail network. Stations in the outlying districts seemed to have been placed in the worst possible positions, well away from the most heavily populated centres. Looking at a railway map of late-nineteenth-century Wigan, the interlacing network of lines demonstrates clearly how a golden opportunity – for giving the town an organised and integrated transport network – was completely thrown away by the railway builders and their lack of co-operation among themselves. It was left to the pioneering tramway companies, and then to the Corporation itself, to develop and exploit a system which would actually benefit the people.

*A gigantic steam hammer at the Wigan Coal and Iron Company*

**Above** – *Blast furnaces at Wigan Coal and Iron Co..*
**Below** – *The stage coach was the only means of travel outside the town.*

# Wigan Pier

IGAN has lived with jokes about the town and the pier for the best part of a century. Today, however, the town has turned the joke into a highly popular and successful tourist enterprise. The jokes that once embarrassed Wigan are now being put to good and productive use. Tradition has it that George Formby Snr. – the father of the 'cleaning windows' George – popularised the idea of Wigan Pier, although he perhaps did not invent it. According to Robert Taylor, one-time stationmaster at Wigan, a group of miners returning by train from Southport in 1891 are believed to have been stopped at signals just outside the town. Across the boggy land by the side of the railway they could see part of an overhead gantry which carried coal trucks from Lamb & Moore's Meadow Pit to Newtown. This was an endless-chain wagonway with a winding hut at a dog leg in its length. From where the train stood, the miners could only see part of the elevated railway – on trestles, and with the little winding house looking for all the world like the pavilion at the end of a seaside pier. 'Where are we!' asked one miner . . . 'Wigan Pier' came the reply, and the idea took hold. The joke was not particularly aimed at Wigan – just at the idea of any northern industrial town, twenty miles inland, being compared with the Victorian elegance of seaside Southport.

*Left: Wigan Pier – the replica pier on its little hump by the canalside. A few feet of track have also been laid to suggest its former use as a wagon tippler.*
*Below: The joke extended to the publication of many postcards like this one, in which a huge electricity pylon is captioned 'the Tower', while the backs of houses in Poolstock bears the legend 'the Promenade'.*
*Right: Demolishing Wigan Pier – taken when the original wagon tippler was removed in 1929.*
*Far right: This way to the Pier – a bit of re-created seaside ephemera inside the modern Heritage Centre.*
*Bottom right: Sunset at Pearsons Flash – another postcard from about 1930.*

Wigan-by-the-Sea    (Sunset Pearsons Flash)

# Royal Visits

HE Ancient and Loyal Borough has had its fair share of royal visits over the years. Since the introduction of photography 150 years ago such visits have been well covered by the town's photographers. From time immemorial, Wigan has been a Royalist town, eagerly celebrating every royal event – so even when royalty did not actually visit the town, bunting and banners, street parties and civic events have marked great royal occasions. Queen Victoria stopped at Wigan once – overnight in the royal train on her way to Scotland. The incessant noise of the ever-busy station apparently disturbed her sleep, so, on future trips north, a quiet siding at Springs was chosen for the royal train to stop. Royal visits have included Edward VII while still Prince of Wales, King George V, Edward VIII while Prince of Wales, King George VI and the present Queen Mother in May 1938, as well as the present Queen. They have all been met with huge crowds and an enthusiastic Wigan reception.

*Above left* – The Prince of Wales arriving at Wallgate Station on 18th May, 1898, en route to Garswood Hall.
*Above right* – The prince at Garswood Hall where he stayed with his friend Lord Gerard.
*Left* – Banners and bunting decorate King Street for Edward VII's Coronation, 1902.
*Opposite* – *top left* – The visit of King George V to Wigan, 1913. The dais was specially constructed for the day.
*– top right* – The King meeting the Mayor on the platform.
*– middle right* – The Prince of Wales – later Edward VIII – at North Western Station.
*– bottom right* – The Duke of Gloucester arriving at Wigan Pier on a barge newly named after him on an official visit to the town in 1934.

Chapter Nine

# Peace and war, war and peace

**Ever since the war, in the complete impossibility of getting houses, parts of the population have overflowed into supposedly temporary quarters in fixed caravans. Wigan, for instance, with a population of about 85,000 has round about 200 caravan dwellings with a family in each – perhaps somewhat near 1,000 people in all ground on which the caravans have been dumped like rubbish shot out of a bucket. Some of then are actually gypsy caravans, but very old ones and in bad repair. The majority are old single decker buses (the rather smaller buses of ten years ago) which have been taken off their weeels and propped up with struts of wood. Some are simply wagons with semi-circular slats on top, over which canvas is stretched, so that the people inside have nothing but canvas between them and the outer air . . . the dirt and congestion of these places is such that you cannot well imagine it unless you have tested it with your own eyes and more particularly your nose . . . It is almost impossible to sleep on the floor, because the damp soaks up from below. I was shown mattresses which were still wringing wet at eleven in the morning.**

George Orwell, *The Road to Wigan Pier* (1937)

 F the nineteenth century was a time of immense progress in the industrial fortunes of the town, it was also peppered with accidents and setbacks, some of which, like the Maypole, made the national news media. It was a period during which the good and the bad vied with each other for the public's attention.

Whilst the most enduring event of the 1870s, for instance, was the opening of the splendid new Market Hall – designed by a Mr John Hunter and built at a cost of £16,000 – and the clearing away of the open stalls in Wallgate, Hallgate and Market Place, the town also figured in the news as a result of a major disaster.

In August 1873 a terrible railway disaster at North Western Station cost the lives of twelve people – from first-class to third-class – when a train jumped the rails and ran along the platform, tipping some of the coaches over the edge of the bridge on to small factories below. *The Illustrated London News* carried extensive illustrated coverage of the disaster – probably the first time Wigan had been featured in its pages.

Twenty years earlier, in 1853, the magazine had run a major illustrated story from Wigan, but of an entirely different nature. In industrial relations, the progress in output had not been achieved without its problems. For the first time, in the second half of the

*An engraving of the scene outside the Royal Hotel after the riots of 1853.*

century, strikes broke out. Several of the strikes became somewhat violent affairs. In 1853 and 1861 demonstrations which had started out as peaceful marches degenerated into trouble. Several more followed in the 1870s and 1880s.

Mining wages, unlike living costs, had by 1853 hardly risen in twenty years, despite huge profits being made by Wigan's increasingly large number of pits. While there was variation from mine to mine, the average a miner could hope to earn was around one shilling and five pence (7p) per ton of coal cut. These were the days before wages as such. Men were paid solely on the amount of coal they cut, shifted, or whatever other job they did. If they did not work, they did not get paid.

*Market Place in the 1870s. Fish and fruit stalls were still sited here, and their produce was used as ammunition by the rioting miners!*

The miners, after trying peaceably to get an increase of about eight per cent on the current rates, withdrew their labour. Whilst that meant that they did not get paid, it also meant no profits for the mine owners.

A march by the miners through the centre of the town on November 4th 1853, aimed at driving home their case, developed into what was described as a riot which resulted in troops being brought into the town from Manchester to assist the police in restoring order. Buildings in Market Place, Wallgate and Queen Street were damaged, market stalls destroyed and, for a time, anarchy ruled in the middle of the town. The main focus of attention was the Royal Hotel and the Eagle & Child public house attached to it. It was in the Royal Hotel that the mine owners met to discuss the miners' claims.

*The Illustrated London News* wrote of the riot:

*A great amount of damage was done to property and for four hours a mob held complete possession of the place. . . . a meeting of mine owners took place in the Royal Hotel and when it broke up, several hundred miners had assembled hoping the masters would have compromised the dispute by consenting to give an advance of one penny to the shilling. When the men learned the masters had only decided to throw open their pits for the men to go to work at the same prices as they came out at, they seemed much disappointed and showed an uneasy feeling.*

When the mine owners left the building, they were pursued by the mob, some of whose more agitated spirits picked up fruit and vegetables from the stalls in the Market Place and started throwing them. In 1853, twenty-four years before the Market Hall was built, Market Place was still the major venue for open-air fruit, vegetable and fish stalls. The violence escalated, as windows were broken, buildings damaged and several people injured.

Troops arrived from Manchester to restore order, but the peace which was achieved was short-lived. When the men heard that the Earl of Crawford was bringing in Welsh miners to work the Haigh pits, trouble broke out again. Although the dispute was eventually settled in the miners' favour, industrial relations were more than a little strained for some time.

As for the Royal Hotel, although it suffered considerable damage in the 1853 strike, it was quickly repaired. It was extensively altered and refurbished – almost out of recognition – in the late 1880s in the years before Station Road was opened up in 1892 to create access to the newly built Central Station. It was demolished in the late 1920s when the site was redeveloped for Woolworths; it is now a branch of John Menzies.

In 1889, the Miners Federation of Great Britain was established, aiming to bring together the various miners' representative groups that had been set up over the years. From then on, miners sought to further disputes as a single national voice. There was a major strike in 1893 which brought virtually all local pits to a standstill. This time the strike was over a proposed cut by the mine owners of 25% in wages, rather than a claim for more pay by the miners. This time some Scottish workers were brought in to work the coal, but eventually the miners won a return to work at the rates of pay in force when the strike started.

Further major strikes followed in 1912 and 1921, and, of course, it was a strike by miners in 1926 that led to the National Strike of that year. In 1912, as in 1853, troops were brought into the town to restore law and order as striking miners went on the rampage.

In the 1893 strike, hardship was widespread, with a large proportion of the town's workforce out of work. Not only the miners suffered; local shops and businesses which relied on their custom also felt hard times. Local churches set up soup kitchens and fed starving children throughout the five months of the dispute. Without such charity, many lives might have been lost through starvation.

The town – like every other town in the land – celebrated Victoria's Golden Jubilee in 1887, and her Diamond Jubilee in 1897 with bunting in the streets, street parties and civic celebrations. The 'Ancient & Loyal Borough' loved to celebrate royal events, even if the monarch was unaware of the fact. The Queen, in all her sixty-four years on the throne, never made an official visit to the town, although she passed through it on many occasions in her royal train. Her son, the Prince of Wales, later Edward VII, did pay two official visits to the town in 1873 to open the Infirmary, and again in the closing years of the century – although he too never visited Wigan while on the throne.

The century closed with Britain at war in South Africa – a war which claimed several local lives. The Boer War lasted from 1899 until 1902 and led to the erection in 1903 of the town's first war memorial, designed by Goscombe John and erected in a central position in front of the pavilion in Mesnes Park. The memorial, consisting of a bronze figure of a soldier on top of a stone plinth, became a common backdrop for groups of soldiers being photographed in later years as they left for future and much more global wars. Today only the base remains in position.

1903 saw the completion and formal opening of the new Mining and Technical College in its splendid Library Street building, now being converted to become the new town hall and library. The Mining College had developed out of the Wigan Mechanics Institute, with a history dating back to the mid-1850s, and one of the first in the country. Local worthies established the first classes for the town's aspiring craftsmen in the old Public Hall in 1856 and one gentleman, Canon Fergie, offered his services – but with conditions. In a letter dated December 1856 he wrote:

> *The attention manifested by many of the young men at the Mechanics Institution and their evident determination to advance themselves intellectually pleased me much, and disposes me to say that I would most willingly sacrifice one evening per week, as well as the time requisite for preparation, to their improvement. I am however in a strait. I am most willing to breast the rain and storm of winter during the evenings I attend the Institution, but neither Mrs Fergie nor myself think it would be very comfortable for me to be knocked down, robbed or garrotted. Already a highway robbery has been committed near here [Pemberton], and sometime since, we heard of garrotting in the neighbourhood of Warrington Lane. Now it strikes me if the young men are very anxious for my instruction, and I very willing to walk to and from Wigan for their sakes, they in turn would, perhaps, have no objection to see me safely home – two at a time – so that they would be company for each other on their return.*

Wigan in the 1850s does not sound as though it was a very safe place for gentlemen of the cloth to walk abroad at night!

The new Library Street building was the college's second home in

**Left** – *Shopping, Victorian-style. A butcher's shop in Scholes, photographed in the 1870s. Carcasses hanging on hooks open to the street were commonplace. The condition the meat must have been in after a day's traffic had run up and down the dusty road outside the shop hardly bears thinking about!*

**Below** – *Oyster Saloon & Supper Bar, The Weind c.1900. The framed notice above the open stall describes the various types of oysters, prawns and other seafood available, together with an advertisement extolling the virtues of tripe. The sign to the immediate left of the male figure advertises a patent oyster opener.*

*Marks & Spencers' Penny Bazaar, Makinsons Arcade, 1925. Marks opened a stall on Wigan Market in early 1891, and for a time lived in the town. It is interesting to notice that the product range – general commodities such as metal buckets, picture frames, crockery and 'practical working clothes at lower than trade prices' – is a long way from the company's present-day image. Although still known as 'Penny Bazaars' at the time this picture was taken, there are items at half a crown in the window.*

*Gent's Outfitters & Pawnshop, Market Place, c.1910. Wilson & Hardwood of 28 Market Place styled themselves as 'Clothiers, Pawnbrokers, Jewellers and Working Men's Providers' and their shop was close to the corner of Market Place and Market Street.*

**Above** – *The Douglas Tavern stood on the corner of Chapel Lane and Millgate, an area unrecognisable today because of redevelopment. This picture dates from the turn of the century. Note the advertisement hoardings.*

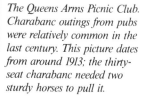

*The Queens Arms Picnic Club. Charabanc outings from pubs were relatively common in the last century. This picture dates from around 1913; the thirty-seat charabanc needed two sturdy horses to pull it.*

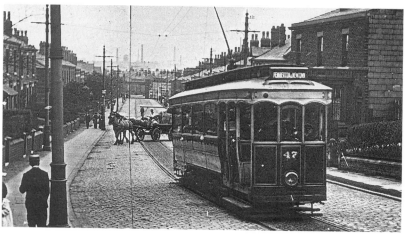

*A Hurst Nelson car, No. 47, in service on the Newton to Pemberton run in about 1906.*

the street – the first having been in a small wood and corrugated iron building further down the street – a site later to be developed as the Pavilion Theatre in 1909 and currently occupied by the swimming pool. The splendid new college building was, for its day, lavishly equipped with:

> *in addition to the usual lecture theatres and class rooms for Science and Art, large drawing offices, separate laboratories for mining, chemistry, metallurgy, physics; and workshops for engineering, plumbing, woodwork, carpentry and joinery, and wood carving.*

It was opened by the Countess of Crawford in January 1903 and served the college well for eighty-five years, although the educational needs of the town outgrew the building many years ago. Despite the addition of an extension which almost doubled its size, the Library Street building was already too small for the college's needs by the early 1950s. The college expanded into the Parsons Walk premises nearly thirty years ago, and into many other sites around the town in the '60s and '70s. Most recently, the Gidlow Mills complex, once a major textiles mill, has been converted for college use. From the humble beginnings of a few evening students in the 1850s, Wigan College of Technology as it became known had more than ten thousand full and part-time students by the mid-1970s.

The official key, presented to the Countess after the opening and given back to the borough at the time Haigh Hall was closed and its contents sold, was made of solid gold, enamelled with the Crawford Arms and set with sapphires and pearls. Lady Crawford added another equally impressive key to her collection when the Pemberton Carnegie Library was officially opened in 1907. By the time the contents of the hall were disposed of, there was a considerable collection of keys, trowels and other items used at official ceremonies. They were all given to the borough.

Andrew Carnegie had donated £5,000 in 1902 for the building of the library and, although he was not present at the opening, he did visit the town in 1909 to be granted the freedom of the borough by the mayor, Alderman Woods.

While a splendid series of photographs survives to commemorate Carnegie's visit to the town, such visual evidence is denied us of the great fire which engulfed part of Market Street in the same year, and of Wigan's water polo team who, in 1909, became English champions!

In 1910, Wigan marked the opening of a building which was to play an even more significant role in the town's future years – the first Board of Trade labour exchange, opened in Woodcock Street in April. The idea behind the labour exchange was to extend job opportunities for the unskilled worker – local union branch secretaries had for decades attempted to find work for time-served men in their membership but, for the unskilled and semi-skilled without the power and influence of a union behind them, things were not so easy.

Mr E. Woodcock, Secretary of the Local Trades Council remarked at the opening that his council 'welcomed any organisation that would help to mitigate the effects of unemployment in the town' – some things apparently never change!

The diversity of employment within the town was increasing, however, into some rather unexpected areas – under the direction of

Mr A. Worswick, Motoplane Ltd. of Gathurst unveiled its first production aircraft in the same month that the labour exchange opened!

The new workhouse infirmary at Billinge, erected by the Wigan union, also opened its doors in 1910, with over eight hundred beds, including special wards set aside for vagrants. In the local press, it was described as a fine example of 'the Poor Law system of the future'.

Events in that year were, however, dominated by the death of King Edward VII in May, and the accession of George V. Local newspapers made much of repeating news stories from the closing years of the last century when, as Prince of Wales, the late King had visited the town – and been photographed by leading professional photographer William Millard. Pictures of the Royal Albert Edward Infirmary carried captions reminding Wiganers that theirs was the only such institution to bear the late King's name. At a civic gathering in the Market Square, the accession of the new King was proclaimed to the townspeople and, at a time which coincided precisely with the royal funeral, the mayor and council processed from the town hall in King Street to the parish church. Previously, at a special meeting of the council, a decision had been made to send a wreath in the shape of a cross to the palace from the people of the ancient and loyal borough.

Suitably regal civic events were also arranged for the coronation of the new King, and loyal greetings again sent from the mayor and corporation. This was rewarded in 1913 with a royal visit to the town by the King and Queen, when once again the Market Square became the focus of attention within the town.

On a domestic level, severe thunderstorms damaged houses in Delph Street and in Mesnes Terrace – between Hope Street and Mesnes Street – a corporation steam-roller vanished into a gigantic hole in the road sufficiently deep, we are told, that no part of it was visible from above!

An announcement in the local press stated that a new Opera House and People's Palace, with a seating capacity of 3,000 was planned for Station Road on a site 'adjacent to the Palatine Mineral Water Works in Market Place'. This proposed addition to the town's theatres and halls prompted the Wigan Entertainment Company to advertise the fact that under their management there were already three fine theatres in the town – the Court with 2,500 seats, the Hippodrome with 2,750 and the Pavilion in Library Street with a capacity of 3,000 and 'adapted for Public Meetings, Dances, Concerts, Pictures and Circuses!'

Just two weeks after the declaration of war in 1914, their summer camp plans replaced by the real thing, the Wigan Territorials assembled in the Drill Hall to make their final preparations for war. They left Wigan on August 20th. Two days later, *HMS Amphion* was sunk at sea. On board was a Wigan-born stoker, who became the first celebrity of the war in the local papers. Less than two months later, the town was welcoming back the first of its wounded, for treatment at Woodlands Hospital in Wigan Lane and at Garswood Hall, hastily converted into a temporary military hospital.

The first real panic of the war came in mid-October when it was claimed that a Zeppelin was over the town preparing to bomb Wigan's factories. Officials discounted the claim, stating that it was not the lights of a Zeppelin, but a meteorite which could be seen as a bright light moving across the night sky. The following day, October 14th, the meteorite was indeed found – in Appley Bridge.

Wigan was deemed to be sufficiently far north to be safe from German attack – safe enough, indeed, to become the temporary home of hundreds of Belgian refugees, who arrived at Hindley in late October and remained in the area for the duration.

Events have a habit of coming together in a strange way – and this was demonstrated no more clearly than the funeral of Wigan's first casualty of the war, on November 14th 1914, the day after a rousingly jingoistic recruiting meeting at the Pavilion had encouraged hundreds of local men and youths to take the King's shilling. In April of the following year, Lord Crawford himself joined up – as a private soldier in the Royal Army Medical Corps.

The sinking of the *Lusitania* provoked mass outrage – and a gathering of thousands in the Market Square in May demonstrated just how strongly the people of Wigan felt about the colossal loss of life. Future gatherings were smaller in scale but became increasingly frequent as over the next three years the people of Wigan gathered together almost weekly to bury their dead from the battlefields of Europe.

Public holidays were abandoned in the town's factories as the demand for war equipment, munitions and clothing grew inexorably. Recruitment reached a peak in 1916, depleting the labour force considerably in the process. Rather than the middle years of the war being punctuated by stories of mass production, of industrial harmony in a common cause, however, in Wigan at least it was punctuated by the most comprehensive catalogue of industrial unrest the town had seen. The tramway employees went on strike in 1915, followed by the miners, the cloggers and the bakers. They were followed by bricklayers' labourers, colliery stokers and engine-men, and, in the mills, the card room operatives and both ring and twist spinners.

While all this was going on, more and more young men were leaving for the front and, in the late spring of 1916, the first group of conscientious objectors were put on trial in the local courts for refusing to 'do their duty'.

As food shortages nationally became more acute, the King issued a statement to be read in all churches in the land in May 1917, 'enjoining frugality in the use of bread'. While there was adequate food in the town, the local vicars, priests and ministers, all did their duty and read the proclamation.

The war was relatively remote from the town, except in so far as local men were fighting and dying, and local industry was almost entirely turned towards supplying the needs of the armies. Yet some unexpected decisions were taken during its four years. While public holidays had been denied to the workforce in 1915 and 1916 because of the need to maximise war production, 1917 marked the beginning of a Wigan tradition – the introduction of local trade holidays. From August 6th 1917, Wigan effectively closed down for three days. In 1919, and subsequently, the holiday was extended to a week.

By the autumn, food shortages were beginning to be felt in the area,

# Entertainment

I N the days before theatres and cinemas, Wiganers made their own entertainment – concerts, outings and so on. Sport has always figured largely in the town and Wigan Rugby League Club – known more accurately as Wigan Football Club – retains a following that makes the rest of the league look unpopular by comparison! Theatres, music halls and cinemas proliferated in the town in the early years of this century, but nearly all have now gone. *The Ritz* continues as the only town centre cinema when in the past there were getting on for a dozen. Only the *Little Theatre* continues the tradition of live entertainment. All the others have been demolished. *The Hippodrome* occupied the site of the TSB in King Street and opposite was the *Palace. The County* still stands further up the street – now a club. Other cinemas and theatres in Library Street, the Weind and elsewhere have also been demolished as audiences dwindled.

*Left:* The Old Dog Music Hall – *Many Music Halls were situated in large rooms of town centre pubs. They offered a variety of cheap – and often bawdy – entertainment.*

*Above: Wigan Excelsior Cycling Club c1900 pose at the gates to Mesnes Park.*

*Left: Mesnes Park, little changed since this turn-of-the-century postcard view, is still one of the most popular places in the town.*

*Right, top: Silcock's Fair on the Market Square – for years this was a regular feature of the Wigan calendar. Fairs had been held on this site for centuries.*

*Right: Markstown Pierrots – a group of scouts putting on a concert party at the turn of the century.*

*Far right: A Tug-of-War between men from neighbouring collieries.*

The Park, Wigan

# Wigan in the Great War, 1914-18

T HERE had never been a war like it before, Wigan men flocked to the recruiting rallies and 'took the King's shilling'. At home, many of the town's factories were turned quickly to war work and Wigan women who had never worked before in their lives joined the hundreds of working women to help with the war effort. A sense of civic pride – and pride in their activity – brought groups together for local professional photographers. The park steps, just in front of the pavilion, might have been built for the purpose – perfect tiering, good lighting, and room for all but the largest of workforces to assemble. The Boer War soldier waved his flag above the heads of many such groups before peace returned.

*Left: A group of Munitions Workers – in front of the group are the shells and mortars that they manufactured. The male managers are in the front row, but the workforce is predominantly women.*

*Shell cases were made at another factory in the town – seen here (**opposite, top left**) in front of their creators. Many of these women may have come from other industries, but many more had never worked before the war effort called upon them.*
*Below: Officers of Wigan Territorials chose the drill hall as the backdrop for their group portrait.*
*Right: The unveiling in 1925 of Wigan's War Memorial, designed several years earlier by Giles Gilbert Scott.*

*Top, right:* Wigan Volunteer Corps pose for the camera before leaving for the war and for action in May 1916.

*Right:* Comrades of the Great War Concert Party – one of a long list of fund-raising groups active during and immediately after the war.

and a Food Control Committee was formed to supervise its distribution and consumption. After only a few weeks of operation, food regulations were tightened significantly, and, by the end of the year, the first of several local tradesmen were prosecuted and heavily fined for breaches of the trading and distribution rules.

Local life went on much as it always had done, however, and a well-reported event in the closing months of the war concerned the death in the town of three cows – killed by bolts of lightning in Wigan Lane!

A civic gathering in the town in August marked the fourth anniversary of the war in 1918 – but an even larger one three months later marked the end, both of the war and of the restrictions it had placed on Wiganers. While the town looked forward to the first 'Peace Christmas' for five years, a cotton strike left thousands of workers in hardship over the festive season. It was just the latest chapter in a five-year period of industrial unrest.

The Belgian refugees left for home in the early months of 1919 after over four years of enforced exile, although the conditions to which they returned can only be guessed at, for Belgium had seen some of the heaviest and most destructive fighting. The Corporation announced that, somehow, a German machine gun had come into its possession. What happened to it afterwards is lost somewhere in the mists of time!

The Territorials, colours in front of their much depleted number, marched back into Wigan in April 1919 – an event which in many ways marked the end of Wigan's war. Events which had been suspended since the summer of 1914 were reinstated – May Queens, Rose Queens, Carnivals, Church Walking Days and so on were all held again. Wigan Cricket Club was re-established and played its first match, and in most respects life returned to normal, except that the summer was punctuated with several ceremonies to unveil war memorials – at Platt Bridge, at Standish Collieries, at Wigan Golf Club and in Bickershaw. Wigan's own war memorial, planned since 1917 and designed by Sir Giles Gilbert Scott, was not completed until 1925. Despite the absence of a memorial, the people of Wigan remembered their dead, and staged massive 'No More War' rallies more than once on the Market Square.

In the interim, industrial change in the town had progressed. The first of the great colliery complexes to close – Douglas Bank – ceased production in 1920, the same year that Vulcanite opened its first factory in Wigan. The factories, forges and mills which had fed the war returned to their peacetime production, but post-war Britain was much less prosperous than before. It was not just collieries which closed – the first mill closures followed quickly after the end of the war, bringing new hardships to the town.

The 1920s and '30s were decades of very mixed fortune for Wigan. Whilst in some areas of activity the town seemed to prosper, the lot of the working people which had improved so significantly in the years before the Great War, regressed considerably. Part of this was an effect of post-war depression in industrial demand which caused widespread unemployment, but equally as worthy of note was the state of the town itself. Wigan, like so many other industrial towns which had been developed during the nineteenth century, now had outdated housing stock, outdated factories and an infrastructure which was already showing its age.

The heavily populated centre of the town had degenerated into a slum of considerable squalor, and the Corporation was engaged in wholesale redevelopment and rehousing. The 1920s and '30s were, with the possible exception of the '60s, the most active periods of housing development seen not just in Wigan but in the country as a whole.

That redevelopment also caused problems among the very group of people it was trying to help. While new housing freed them from the insanitary and in many cases unsafe slums in which they had lived hitherto, it also increased the costs of the families who were rehoused at a time when they were perhaps least able to afford it.

Average rents in town centre slums in 1930 were about four shillings a week – 20p – whereas the new council housing in Whelley, Beech Hill and elsewhere cost over twice that amount. Add to that considerable increase in rents, the cost of bus fares to work – where buses were available – and the effects were often quite considerable.

George Orwell, in *The Road to Wigan Pier,* recounts some diary entries he made during his stay in Wigan in the 1930s, and these highlight the problem. He visited a house in Wallgate – one up, one down, with a space under the stair which doubled as kitchen and coal hole. An outside lavatory was fifty yards away and the total cost, including borough rates, was 7/3d (36p) per week. It had no garden, of course, and shared a common yard at the front. In Beech Hill he found a Corporation house with kitchen, hall and living room downstairs, two large and one small bedrooms upstairs, a bathroom with hot and cold water and an inside toilet – vastly superior accommodation which also had a good-sized and well-tended garden, but which, with rates, cost the family 11/3d (56p) per week. Added to that was 4d per day bus fares into town, so the house in total represented a cost of 80p per week – more than double the Wallgate slum. Another council house in Whelley – where gardens were overgrown and the estate was already by 1936 looking rather run down – cost 10/3d but had an outside toilet and no bus service into the town centre. While the Beech Hill tenants were happy with their lot, the Whelley ones were apparently not!

The Corporation was constantly extending its passenger services, both with trams and with buses. The electrification of the tramways had started in the opening years of the century, and through the first quarter of the century, the network was extended and many of the narrow gauge lines were converted to standard gauge. One of the last lines to go to the broader track was with the Aspull–Wigan route, finally converted in 1923, just two years before trolley buses appeared in the town for the first time.

Some pioneering ideas were tried out by Wigan Corporation Tramways – including a 1925 experiment of having posting boxes on some of the most heavily used vehicles!

Wigan never took to trolley buses – only four were bought, and they only ran for a few years on the Martland Mill route, being withdrawn in 1931 along with most of the trams. The bus – first introduced just after the First World War – became the Corporation's sole mode of public transport.

The 1920s and '30s saw many features which are part of the modern town being introduced. For example, King Street became one-way as early as 1927 – the same year the Royal Arcade opened for business – and 1930 saw the introduction of 'robot policemen' – the first traffic lights – at the junction of Mesnes Street and Standishgate. 1935 saw the first of sixty-six planned pedestrian crossings – complete with Belisha Beacons – introduced.

Politically, many things were changing as well. With the defeat of the Conservative Government in January 1924 – as a result of the first Lib-Lab pact – the country's first Labour prime minister, Ramsay MacDonald, took up office. In his cabinet, as Secretary of State for War, Ince's MP Stephen Walsh became both the town's first government minister, and a privy councillor. His cabinet career was, however, short-lived, as in the general election of October 1924 the Conservatives were again returned to power – albeit with fewer Members of Parliament – and remained in office until 1929. Walsh himself continued in the Commons until January 1929, completing twenty-three years as Ince's MP, as well as, in 1927, assuming the presidency of the Lancashire and Cheshire Miners' Federation. He retired from politics through ill-health and died two months later, in March 1929. Such was the respect for him in the town that his funeral became a major civic event, with military escort, and the mayor and council in procession behind the hearse.

Before a by-election could be held to fill the vacant Ince seat, the Conservatives went to the country and in the May '29 election, Labour was returned to power with a manifesto committed to world peace, disarmament and a return to full employment. They remained in office until the first national government of 1931. Their three major policies were to prove ironically unsuccessful. The '30s were over-shadowed by the worst unemployment and poverty the country had seen, by massive rearmament, and by preparations for war.

It is often somewhat surprising to the modern researcher when confronted with the early history of this century, to realise just how great recent technological progress has been. As an example, when the 1924 Empire Exhibition at Wembley was opened – intended to stimulate trade between Britain, the Empire and the rest of the world – radio was still in its infancy. Thus, when King George V's opening speech was broadcast, very few of the British people had the equipment to receive it. In Wigan, a radio receiver was set up in the Market Square and the speech broadcast through loudspeakers. A considerable crowd gathered in the square to hear their King.

While the exhibition may have painted a healthy picture of British industry to visitors in London, the same was not true in hundreds of towns throughout the country. In Wigan, in addition to the Douglas Bank Colliery closure already mentioned, Tayleur and Meadow pits, and several others all closed during the first few years of the 'twenties. The number of miners out of work increased steadily, and the wages and conditions of those in work got poorer and poorer. The miners' strike of 1926, and the short-lived national strike which grew out of it are both well documented in histories of the period. In Wigan, they added to the already considerable hardship.

Out of unemployment and poor housing conditions often comes malnutrition and disease. Poor Houses, Workhouses, soup kitchens and other aspects of poverty – organised and managed by the Wigan

Poor Law Union and by local churches – did what they could to alleviate the worst of the suffering, but for disease there was no easy remedy. While the medical welfare of the poor was subsidised in a variety of ways, it still cost money to be ill, and with outbreaks of diseases such as smallpox – recorded in the town in 1927 and again in 1937 – there was little medical science of the day could do. Added to that were the recurrent diseases of the northern industrial town – silicosis, pneumoconiosis and tuberculosis – symptoms of the climate and the working conditions. The Wrightington Tuberculosis Hospital opened its doors in 1933 and found no shortage of patients.

Leisure activities in towns like Wigan developed considerably during the latter half of the nineteenth century and the early years of the present. Mention has already been made of the provision of theatres – and to these can be added a considerable number of small music halls, usually located in large rooms behind pubs. Of pubs themselves, there were hundreds. And Woodhouse Greyhound Stadium opened in 1928 – the town's first, but not apparently its last, for in March 1933 the Empress Hall hosted a large protest meeting against 'the uncontrolled increase in dog racing tracks in the town!'

Cinemas opened in several areas of the town – large buildings in the town centre and smaller ones in the outskirts, often seating three or four hundred people and sited near housing estates. In the centre of town, theatres were converted for film rather than live performances. The first 'talkie' was shown in the County Playhouse in King Street in 1928, and in 1930, after closure due to falling attendances as a theatre, the Court reopened as a cinema, surviving in that role until the 1970s. The Ritz – the sole survivor today – opened in March 1937.

The dual problems of poverty and unemployment haunted the town during the 'thirties – hunger marchers on their way to Preston passed through Wigan in November 1933, and the unemployed marched from Wigan to London in the following year.

The Corporation sent a deputation to the Minister of Labour in March 1935 to seek help for the five thousand miners who were currently out of work. For five thousand miners to be out of work during the winter of 1934-5 meant that even more would be laid off in the spring as demand for fuel lessened.

In the summer of 1936, out of a population of 87,000, and a workforce of about 36,000, over 12,000 were on the dole. As Orwell pointed out in *The Road to Wigan Pier,* as each person drawing the dole probably supported at least two others, something approaching forty per cent of the people of Wigan were dependent upon dole money for their survival. Of that 12,000, some sixty per cent had been unemployed since the end of the previous decade.

During 1935 and 1936, even more mines, mills and factories closed as demand slumped – the last blast furnaces at Top Place were demolished in the spring of 1936, and in the September of that year, Pemberton Colliery installed a machine at the Pit Brow to screen the coal, putting the last of the pit lasses out of work as well.

Some of the unemployed were given work by the Corporation – but a small proportion. Council-house building continued throughout the slump and, at a cost of £6,000, the new bus station was completed in the Market Square and opened in April 1936.

In an attempt to lighten the diet of bad news, the local press carried a story in October 1936 of the sighting of that most spectacular of ornithological events, a Rooks' Parliament, at Wrightington.

The period since the Great War had not proved to be very comfortable for the majority of Wiganers. While the wealthy had been largely cushioned from the hardhips and the uncertainty of the two decades since the Armistice, the full weight of slump and depression had fallen on the shoulders of the workforce. In September 1938, with the arrival of large supplies of civilian gas-masks in the town, the preparations had already started for the outbreak of war a year later.

On September 1st 1939, the evacuation of children from Manchester and Salford was commenced, with a large number being moved the few miles to the presumed safety of Wigan. A total of one hundred and thirty-three thousand people were moved out of the city – including children, pregnant mothers, the old and the infirm. 46,000 were moved on that first day – with about six hundred coming to Wigan. Over one hundred special trains left Manchester during that day.

On the day after the outbreak of war, September 4th 1939, theatres, cinemas, dance halls and sports stadiums were closed – it was originally stated that they would remain closed for the duration, but common sense later prevailed and cinemas and theatres were reopened, as long as patrons carried their gas-masks. The street lights went out for six years, however, and Wigan prepared for war.

In all, the Manchester Education Committee which master-minded the children's evacuation, located over one hundred and seventy-five thousand billets for the evacuees in Lancashire, Cheshire, Derbyshire and Yorkshire before the official exodus began.

The wisdom of the move was amply demonstrated in December 1940 when the Manchester blitz started. Large areas of the city were flattened by successive air-raids, but no bombs reached Wigan less than twenty miles away. Six hundred bombs fell on the city, changing its appearance for ever. When those children left Wigan in 1945 to return to their homes, the city centre that they knew was a flattened bomb site.

Wigan's first casualty of the war was recorded on September 23rd 1939, and its first panic on November 11th after an electrical fault accidentally set off the air-raid sirens at eleven in the morning. The official test of the alarms – on December 15th – was well advertised in advance and caused no panic whatsoever! The year closed in silence – for the first time since 1917-18, the parish church bells did not ring in the new year. The twenty-year peace which was to have endured forever had ended. They did not ring in the new year again until 1946 – although, by special dispensation, the bells were rung to welcome Christmas Day in 1941.

Many other restrictions and ordinances were introduced very quickly. Cyclists were required to have hooded rear lights on their bicycles and, for motorists, a single grade of petrol – Pool Petrol as it was called – was introduced. The Secretary of State for Mines, reported in the *Manchester Guardian* for Monday September 4th, announced that there were good supplies of petrol in the country which would be available, on ration from September 16th, at 1/6d (7.5p) per gallon.

Speaking from his study in Buckingham Palace on the evening of

September 3rd, King George VI had warned that this second global war would be very different from the first. The rise of aerial warfare meant that towns as far removed from the main theatre of war as Wigan was, were now under threat.

The King's speech concluded:

*The task will be hard. There will be dark days ahead, and war can no longer be confined to the battlefields, but we can only do the right as we see the right, and reverently commit our cause to God. If one and all we keep resolutely faithful to it, ready for whatever service or sacrifice it may demand, then with God's help we shall prevail. May he bless and keep us all.*

Throughout the first few weeks of the war, the dramas and the losses were individual – Wigan's second casualty was named as Ezekial Livesay of Wallgate, and serving in the navy. The third and fourth were a mother and child lost in a ship sunk after a U-boat attack. As the war progressed and the numbers multiplied, deaths and funerals would become too common for each to be recorded individually in the pages of the local press. So immediately did the war preoccupy the townsfolk that it was decided not to hold Rememberance Day gatherings for the dead of the Great War in November 1939. By the end of the year, ARP units had been established in the town, there was a battalion of 'Dad's Army' – the Home Guard – and local bodies were actively engaged in raising money to buy Spitfires, cigarettes for the troops, tanks and just about any other item of war equipment of which there was a shortage – and that included most!

With the evacuated children from Manchester and Salford safely housed in Shevington, Parbold and Appley Bridge, Wigan received over seven hundred evacuees from the Channel Islands early in 1940. In 1944 hundreds of London children would also be sent to Wigan where they were given a warm welcome on North Western station platform by the mayor and mayoress, and comfortable homes in the town until peace returned.

Over the Christmas period of the Manchester blitz in 1940, and the several raids on Liverpool, the skies around Wigan were lit up with the fires of the two great cities. The town apparently warranted a mention by Lord Haw-Haw at one point – and there certainly were good reasons why the Germans might have liked to eliminate the munitions works at Beech Hill, or Pagefield Ironworks to name but two. Both were producing munitions ranging from small-bore ammunition to huge shell cases. However, the works remained intact throughout the war and, along with other similar factories in the town, contributed to the general effort.

As far as the local press was concerned, wartime stories ranged from the seemingly endless programme of fund-raising events, and the removal of park and garden railings for re-use in military equipment, through to stories of the imprisonment of a substantial number of townsfolk for a veriety of misdemeanours. These included conscientious objectors who refused to comply with the rules, shopkeepers who failed to comply with the food orders – either selling goods they were not licensed to sell, or selling at inflated prices – and court cases involving the leaders of an apparently thriving black-market!

Punctuating these stories were equally endless mentions of local men whose lives had been lost, of acts of bravery and of the progress of the war from a Wigan angle. Again local stately homes and hospitals received war-wounded, including a number of other Allied nationalities – a group of Poles were entertained by the mayor in April 1945 – but it was not just the allied soldiers who spent part of their war in the town. Both Italian and German prisoners-of-war were brought to the Wigan area for a while, working at Central Wagons Works in Ince.

When, in 1945 towards the end of the war, the Americans arrived, there can have been few of the combatant nationalities who were not represented within the Borough!

If everybody old enough can still remember 'the day war broke out', there may just be a few who cannot recall very much of the night the war ended! Bonfires were lit on many hilltops, the streets were again full of lights, pubs either stayed open or – if they had already closed – reopened, and in every town a hundred impromptu street parties lasted well into the night. Wigan was no exception.

While cities like London, Manchester and Liverpool, badly damaged by German air-raids, had the immediate task of tackling the dereliction, Wigan had no such problem. In many ways that fact – welcome as it was – postponed the emergence of a post-war town, postponed the redevelopment of the poorest housing and the town centre. The soldiers returning to Wigan in 1945 and 1946 returned to a familiar townscape and, with rationing staying in force for almost a decade after the war ended, to shortages and hardships only a little removed from those they had left at the end of the previous decade. The major redevelopment of the town waited for better times.

**Above** – *Farriers at work at Wigan Coal and Iron Co., Top Place, about 1918.*
**Below** – *A Pemberton Colliery wagon decorated for the Pemberton Carnival, 1932.*

**Above –** *A group of millworkers celebrate the coronation of King George VI, Sandbrook Mill, 1937.*
**Below –** *This splendid 'Black 5' locomotive was completely rebuilt at Springs Sheds after it took almost the full impact of a German bomb which had exploded as the train stood at signals near Crewe station. A Springs driver, Fred Mayor, was killed, but the fireman, Reg Tierney, another local man, lived to tell the tale.*

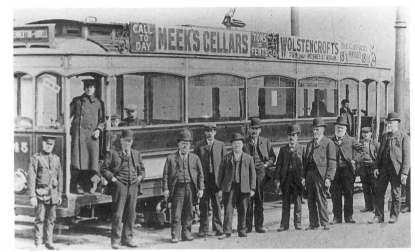

*The first Hurst Nelson tramcar, No. 45, with council officials after its final trial run in 1904, prior to entering regular service.*

*The Edwardian Market Place, splendidly decked out in flags and bunting for the coronation of Edward VII.*

*Fundraising rally on the Market Square to provide money for the blind, 23 July 1916. The Mayor was Alderman S. Hilton. Prominent banners behind him show the breadth of union support enjoyed by the charity.*

Chapter Ten

# Yesterday, today and tomorrow

Wigan lies on the small River Douglas which flows into the estuary of
the Ribble. There is connection by canal with Liverpool, Manchester
etc. The town has coal mines which are famous for cannel coal, and
which employ a large proportion of the inhabitants and supply the
factory furnaces. The chief manufactures are cotton fabrics and linen
fabrics; the town also possesses iron forges, iron and brass foundries,
oil, grease and chemical works, railway wagon factories, and bolt,
screw and nail works.

*Encylopaedia Britannica* (1950)

N many respects, 1950 is only yesterday. Yet in Wigan,
1950 is so long ago that the town then is almost
unrecognisable today. The last four decades have seen
redevelopment and urban renewal on such a vast scale
that a native Wiganer returning to the town after forty
years might easily get lost! This is an interesting – and
widespread – feature of post-war Britain.

Towns which had remained largely unaltered since the nineteenth
century started on a process of renewal in the 1950s and '60s that swept
away almost everything before them. Whilst much of it deserved to go
– the quality of much of the housing and other buildings erected in
late-Victorian Wigan for instance had little to commend it – the
wholesale destruction of many northern towns came perilously close
to leaving a large and irreplaceable gap in their architectural heritage.
While Georgian and earlier architecture was protected, there was a
period in the '50s and '60s when nothing but scorn was poured on
Victorian buildings. Wigan, in starting late along the redevelopment
road, was spared some of the excessive zeal of the planners, while at
the same time ridding itself of the worst relics of its industrial past!

The borough council started where change was most necessary – in
clearing away the slums of Scholes, Wallgate and other early-Victorian
areas of the town, where housing quality and density was of an order
which no civilised community could any longer tolerate. In exercising
that civic responsibility, the borough council changed forever the
Wigan street plan and Wigan skyline.

Earlier in this study, comment was made of the problems encoun-
tered in identifying the exact position and extent of the Roman town,
the Anglian settlement and so on. Those problems are not exclusive to
the earlier civilisations. Today, without the benefit of old maps, it is
impossible for the modern visitor to locate, for example Central

Station – so completely was every trace of it and its approach tracks obliterated by redevelopment in the 1960s. Today its memory survives only in the name of Station Road, whilst its foundations were swept away only a few years ago to be replaced with the Station Road multi-storey car park. The same is true of the nineteenth-century line of Chapel Lane, Millgate and other streets, replaced with an entirely new street plan, first in the '60s with the construction of the swimming pool, and in the '80s with the carving through the town of the ring road.

Some streets have changed very little – or at least it seems that way until comparisons are made with old photographs. Fire has wrought a few changes – like the replacement of Debenham's original Crawford House in the '50s when, as Pendlebury's, the building was completely gutted. Amazingly, looking at today's volume of traffic, Standishgate remained two-way until the early 1970s.

Less than twenty years has passed since there was a policeman on point duty at the junction of Market Street, Wallgate, Library Street and Market Place, and much less than that since the traffic flow was sufficiently light parking to be allowed on both sides of Library Street.

It was in 1963 that my first visit to the town brought me into Wigan Central on a cold, windy evening, and the station, already semi-derelict and decades overdue for modernisation or demolition, presented an image out of the history books. With oil lamps blowing to and fro above the old platforms, my first impressions were not inspiring. Twenty-one years ago, coming to live in the town, it was to the old North Western Station, in the very early hours of yet another wet and windy day, that my overnight train delivered me. The walk through the subways, water dripping from every joint in the roof, and wind howling through the tile-lined tunnels, did – I freely admit – cause me to question the merits of accepting a job in Wigan!

A generation of Wiganers has come of age since we had a last pint in the Commercial, or the Top Legs, or bought a pound of nails in Bolton's shop at the top of Makinson's Arcade. And it is twenty years since the first rumblings of protest were heard about the architecture of the Wigan Centre Arcade and the replacement of the Market Street shops with the famous 'ramp'. Perhaps architecturally the single most inappropriate development the town centre has seen, the Wigan Centre, is now mercifully redeveloped as Marketgate, and along with the massive Galleries project, will become part of a town centre for the twenty-first century.

The scale of change in this decade has been phenomenal – and memories fade so quickly. Were it not for photography, the old Market Square, the old Market Hall, Hope Church, and countless other buildings would already be fading from most people's memories.

Indeed, many once-important 'landmarks' have already been forgotten by all but the older members of society. The Hippodrome was burned down in King Street in April 1956, but for those of us who came to Wigan after that event, the TSB building – or Wigan Savings Bank as it once was – might as well always have been there. It only occupies the Hippodrome site in the minds of those who remember the Hippodrome! Similarly, a complete generation does not remember the Pavilion – knowing instead only the swimming pool – and does not remember the Weind before the cinema/theatre was demolished and the grass was planted. Change is relative, and only nostalgia persists.

Nostalgia, for the Saracens Head, demolished in the path of the top end of the ring road; for the Park Hotel now transported into the Wigan Pier Heritage Centre; and for a hundred other pubs which have gone since the war, may remain for decades to come.

But nostalgia for 'the way we were' *per se* overlooks the squalor and poverty which 'the way we were' imposed on the majority of the towns-people. It is very easy to think longingly back to 'neat little rows of terraced houses' – and conjure up an idyllic scene something like Birkett Bank on a sunny summer's afternoon, so typical of Victorian Wigan – while sitting in a centrally heated house with all 'mod cons'. As a photographer, I would have loved to have been alive in the early-nineteenth century photographing the life and work of the people of a town like Wigan – but I would have needed my car, telephone, computer and central-heating, to name but a few of today's 'necessities' – as well. That is the indulgence nostalgia permits us all. The reality would be much less attractive.

Since the war, the local Borough Council – and since 1974 the Metropolitan Borough Council – has fought hard to bring a wide range of new industries to the town, to replace the older ones which were reaching the end of their time. The quotation which opened this chapter may have been written only four decades ago, but in terms of a description of Wigan as it approaches the end of the twentieth century, it might as well have been written a hundred years ago. The town no longer fits the description even remotely.

Since the war, an aggressive policy of attracting outside industries into the town has been pursued – with a marketing strategy that has developed in sophistication over the years, despite the somewhat ill-conceived 'Modern Wigan has no Peer' and 'Wigan – Hub of the North West' postmarks of the early 'seventies. Today's marketing involves national newspapers and magazines, high profile PR and a team of experts who know that to win the battle against the town's employment problems, the effort must never be diluted.

The older industries survive only as street names or pub names – Moss Pit Row, Brick Kiln Lane, Mill Street, Pottery Road, the Venture Pub and so on – or looking out at us from old photographs. In their place has been introduced a range of industries too extensive to be listed here, while the town's Leisure Department has exploited nostalgia for the past, and a poor music hall joke, and turned the derelict canalside buildings at Wigan Pier into one of the country's leading tourist attractions.

Wigan enters the last decade of the twentieth century poised to accept the challenges of the twenty-first. But amidst all the change, some things remain constant. The people of Wigan may have changed in their expectations of life, but in their down-to-earth, hardworking and friendly nature, they are a constant.

While architecture, history and progress may describe a town, it is the people who are the town. In that respect Wigan is fortunate. In 1936, George Orwell, countering criticisms of his commentary on the town in *The Road to Wigan Pier* stressed that point when he admitted a liking for Wigan – the people, however, and not the place. The place, since Orwell's day, has improved dramatically.

The architecture, the amenities, the social conditions and the opportunities are now much more worthy of the people who live here.

And what of the future? Development necessarily goes hand-in-hand with controversy. The developments on the horizon are no exception and the controversies will be no less vigorous than those surrounding the demolition of the old market hall, the building of the Galleries, the ring road, and a host of other projects that are now accepted and welcome parts of today's Wigan.

A new single hospital for Wigan and Leigh, replacing Wigan, Leigh and Billinge is planned, centralising and – it is claimed – improving facilities. The reverse of the coin, the protestors predict, is a single site inconvenient for most people without transport in a time of reducing public transport services. The new M6-M61 link is also on the horizon, and already a modicum of planning blight is apparent along its proposed routes.

The future of Wigan railway services is also constantly under review and the quality and frequency of trains on both the east-west and north-south lines is already a frequent subject for letters in the local press. The electrification of the east-coast main-line route already threatens the London to Carlisle line to an extent, and when and if, west-coast, north-south services are increasingly routed through Manchester, North Western's future as a main-line station may be re-examined.

The quest for new employment opportunities for the town goes on. New industrial estates are planned, and new industries seem to be arriving in the town with a regularity that many other similar-sized towns must envy. Whether or not a return to full employment is ever possible, and indeed, what form such employment will take, is a secret only the future will reveal.

Wigan's first two thousand years has been peppered with incident, history, and contrasts. There is nothing to suggest that the next two thousand years will be any less interesting.